Writing Realistic D
& Flash Fiction
a Thorough Primer for Writers of Fiction and Essays

by Harvey Stanbrough

Published by Central Avenue Press
Albuquerque, New Mexico

Requests to make copies of any part of the work should be mailed to the following address:
Central Ave. Press 2132-A Central SE #144, Albuquerque, NM 87106

Publisher's Cataloging-in-Publication

Stanbrough, Harvey.
     Writing realistic dialogue and flash fiction: a thorough primer for writers of fiction & essays / Harvey Stanbrough.
       p. cm.
       Includes indes.
       LCCN 2004102562
       ISBN 0-9715344-5-4

     1.Dialoque. 2. Fiction – Authorship,. 3. Essays – Authorship. I. Title.

PN1551.273 2004   808.3'96
                          QBI33-2037

Book design and cover photography by Kyle Zimmerman

Central Ave. Press
2132-A Central SE #144, Albuquerque, NM 87106
www.centralavepress.com
(505) 323-9953

Printed in the United States of America

Dedication

I dedicate *Writing Realistic Dialogue & Flash Fiction* to Writers and Poets, those defenders and innovators of the language who, to all outward appearances, willingly and deliberately engage in this endeavor but who actually couldn't escape its siren song if they tried.

Acknowledgments

This book is a better, more complete work thanks to the invaluable assistance of two friends: Penny Porter, whose notion of the importance of dialogue as a vehicle for emotion served as the cornerstone for Chapter 2, and Dawn Wink (http://www.dawnwink.com), whose enthusiastic support and knack for asking the right questions helped me smooth out the wrinkles. I am in their debt. Special thanks also to Joan Upton Hall (http://www.joanuptonhall.com), Suzanne Spletzer, and Bob Yehling (http://www.wordjourneys.com) for their input.

Thanks to Jason Gurley (http://www.deeplyshallow.com) for the use of an excerpt from his short story, "After a Time" (*Close Program*, Pixel Press, 2000) and to Mac Fallows for the gracious use of a situation from his novel manuscript, *The Search for Gojesmo*. Although some examples are patterned after problems in manuscripts I edited, all other excerpts are taken from my own writing.

Contents

Writing Realistic Dialogue
& Flash Fiction

a Thorough Primer for Writers of Fiction and Essays

Introduction

We often hear readers speak of "memorable dialogue" or "memorable characters" or even "memorable scenes," but in every case, what is memorable is the *emotion* of the dialogue or character or scene, not the dialogue or character or scene itself. Of course, only characters can convey emotion, and their most effective vehicle is dialogue — but not in the common sense of the term. Actually, dialogue is the sum of the stuff between the quotation marks plus the accompanying narrative. After all, how can we convey a sense of emotion without allowing the reader to experience the characters' misery or fear or humor or elation?

Why You Should Buy This Book

Most importantly, you should buy this book because if your dialogue (or narrative, for that matter) does not ring true, the reader will put your book back on the shelf and find something else to read.

In researching the market for *Writing Realistic Dialogue & Flash Fiction*, I noticed that although there are a lot of how-to books out there for writing fiction and nonfiction in general, there aren't many dedicated to the art of crafting realistic dialogue. That surprised me, considering how important dialogue is to excellent fiction and how useful it can be in creative nonfiction.

Of the dialogue books on the shelves, I also noticed that none discuss the use of punctuation as a specific component of realistic dialogue. In the first book in the Thorough Primer series, *Punctuation for Writers* (Central Ave Press, 2003), I went into great detail about punctuation and grammar in general, but only touched on the specifics of the use of punctuation in dialogue. This volume will remedy that oversight.

I also have found no other books on writing fiction or nonfiction that discuss dialogue as a reader-involvement tool. Among the more important characteristics of realistic dialogue is its ability to further suspend a reader's disbelief and directly involve her in the story as an active participant.

Finally, I've seen very few books that discuss flash fiction at all, and none that discuss its relationship to dialogue.

In short, if you want your dialogue to sing, if you want it to attract the reader and then compel him to keep turning pages, if you want to learn how dialogue and narrative and the attendant punctuation conspire to transport the reader into a whole other world — your fictional world — this is the book for you.

What Is Realistic Dialogue?

It might be better to ask What is *unrealistic* dialogue? Plainly put, unrealistic dialogue is any written conversation between two or more characters that simply doesn't sound natural. You probably have heard some of it in writers' critique groups and reading circles, and (unfortunately) you might even have read some of it in published books. If your dialogue sounds forced or stiff or stilted, the reader will pick up on it immediately. From that point forward, he'll be watching for your dialogue gaffes rather than paying attention to (and being absorbed into) your story line.

So realistic dialogue is any non-linear, non-stilted conversation between two or more characters or even, sometimes, between the narrator and the reader. It is what you hear in everyday life but without the boring stuff. Realistic dialogue has the rhythms and spontaneity of everyday speech. It is two or more characters conversing without the fear that some diction teacher will take them by the ear if they say *Yeah* instead of *Yes* or answer a question with something less than a complete, grammatically correct sentence. Most of all, writing realistic dialogue is the art of putting the nuances of language into your character's mouth and the reader's mental ear.

What Is Flash Fiction?

Once again, it might be better to first define what flash fiction is not: It is not an essay, it is not a vignette or slice of life, it is not a prose poem, and it is not simply a story premise. Each of these genres is discussed briefly in Chapter 5.

Flash fiction is a complete short story that involves all four elements of fiction — setting, character(s), conflict, and resolution — in 99 words or fewer. As you might imagine, the successful flash fiction story depends heavily on suggestion or implication. Because of its brevity, flash fiction is an excellent exercise in word economy, and it is also an ideal tool with which writing instructors can illustrate the interaction of the elements of fiction in a limited space.

Flash fiction has been called the most enjoyable anguish a writer can experience in fewer than 99 words. Many writers have thanked me and cursed me in the same sentence for having introduced them to the wonderful enigma that is flash fiction.

Why Present Writing Realistic Dialogue and Writing Flash Fiction Together?

When I present classes or workshops at writers' conferences, I often combine my Writing Realistic Dialogue presentation with my presentation on Writing Flash Fiction. Because of its brevity, flash fiction depends more heavily on implication (or suggestion) and innuendo than do other forms of fiction. Dialogue is an extremely effective vehicle for delivering those nuances, so the combination seemed natural. Also, both realistic dialogue and flash fiction are functions of the nuances of the language.

Finally, flash fiction is such a wonderful tool and such an enjoyable exercise that I wanted to take this opportunity to introduce it to as many writers as possible. In purchasing this book on dialogue, you're getting a two-for-one deal — well, at least one-and-a-half for one.

A Few Notes

1. Many instructors and writers teach dialogue using similar techniques, explanations, definitions, and examples. Except where specifically cited in the text, all ideas, explanations, definitions, and examples in this book are unique and original to me. Any resemblance of any techniques, explanations, definitions, or examples in this book to those presented by any other writers or instructors, orally or in print, is strictly coincidental.

2. The examples, with very few exceptions, are from my own writing. This is by design, but not from some overblown notion regarding the value of my own work over that of someone else. Rather, I use examples mostly from my own fiction, nonfiction, and even poetry so you can see that I actually use the techniques in this book and because I'm certain of the intent of my own work. I don't like trying to explain why another writer does what she does or what she means to accomplish with a particular technique unless I'm certain of it. Finally, even in our litigation-happy society, there is very little chance that I will sue myself.

3. I had the assistance and invaluable advice of several friends in brainstorming and molding this book. They are listed in the acknowledgments. One of them pointed out that much of this text is written in the passive voice, whereas the active voice is better for writing fiction and creative nonfiction. Of course, I fully agree. Furthermore, anyone would be hard pressed to find so much as a passive letter, much less a passive sentence, in my own fiction, poetry, and essays. Because this is a book *about* writing creatively and not a fictional account itself, I hope the reader will forgive the style. I assure you, there are no passive constructions in the examples and excerpts I chose to illustrate various techniques.

4. This is a book about writing dialogue, not the basic process of writing. Nothing here presumes to usurp your writing process. For example, in Chapter 3, I write that

". . . whereas dialogue almost always is necessary because it's being spoken by characters about a situation in the story, with narrative, the writer has the additional albatross of having constantly to decide whether the narrative he's been working on for three hours is necessary at all."

I scattered similar comments throughout the book. One confidant suggests I should clarify these statements by advising you not to ". . . mess up [your] creative flow with these questions until subsequent drafts." I didn't mean to imply that you should stop while writing your narrative and determine immediately which segments of narrative are necessary and which are not. Every writer has his or her own process. Many edit and revise as they go. Many simply write, then edit and revise in a completely separate session. I edit and revise as I write, then fine tune in a separate session . . . or two . . . or three. Whatever your process, follow it.

5. The very nature of creative writing in general and dialogue in specific lends itself to overlapping techniques. To negate the need for in-chapter cross references, I'll tell you now that you will find examples of the same technique in different sections of the book. For example, you will find a discussion and examples of use of the em dash in Chapter 1, Chapter 2, and elsewhere as it seems appropriate. At the risk of boring or offending those of you who have been writing for a longer period of time, I'd rather provide too many examples than too few. At the point where you "get it," simply move on to the next section.

6. Finally, I tried to construct this book so it could be read cover to cover, used as a quick reference, or used as a text book. Each chapter and section stands on its own, but they also follow an ascending sequence. I've provided my definitions of certain terms (in **bold** the first time they appear in the text) in a glossary, and I've also included an index to aid in your search for a particular technique or term.

Chapter 1   Introduction to Dialogue

Show, Don't Tell. This is the admonition on which every writer cuts her teeth. Writers swap this phrase like currency and as if each is coining it for the first time, editors offer it up as original and sage advice, and creative writing teachers base whole semesters around it. In short, everybody talks about it, but few actually explain it. We will explain it in this text.

In Chapter 3, writers are instructed in the liberal use of strong nouns and action verbs, and the limited use of descriptive adjectives and adverbs, to liven up their writing. Briefly, when the reader sees a noun, a mental picture of that noun appears in his mind (that is, he sees it); when the reader sees an action verb, it causes that mental picture to move. The writer, through the use of nouns and action verbs, provides the reader with a mental movie; he shows the reader what is going on rather than simply describing what is going on. When the reader becomes the viewer of that mental movie, he feels he is an active participant in the story rather than a passive observer. When you *show, don't tell* a story with strong, active **narrative**, you engage the reader.

In this chapter, we're going to discuss another, even more effective way to show, don't tell — another way to engage the reader — the effective use of realistic dialogue.

Dialogue Defined

Dialogue is the spoken communication between two or more **characters** or a character's unspoken, internal communication (thought).

A friend, playing devil's advocate as she helped me brainstorm this book, posed these questions: *How much dialogue is too much? When is there not enough?* It would be more appropriate to ask *How much narrative is too much?* or *When is there not enough?* As you'll see repeated throughout this book, even well-written narrative is intrusive, and a strong enough (or unnecessary) intrusion will cause the reader to stop reading every time. If you rattle on with so much as one sentence of unnecessary narrative, you'll lose the reader, probably permanently.

Unlike narrative, *dialogue is never intrusive*. Even weak, stilted dialogue creates within the reader a sense that he's part of the story, and because dialogue is so inviting and accommodating, the reader is very forgiving. You have greater room for error when writing dialogue than when writing narrative. That is not to say poor writing is acceptable, of course; perfection always should be your goal.

The purpose of dialogue, whether well-written and more effective (realistic dialogue) or poorly written and less effective (stilted or convoluted dialogue), is to convey the thoughts of the characters to the reader via that character's spoken communication with one or more other characters or unspoken communication with himself (thought or internal dialogue). Realistic dialogue takes it a step further by conveying those thoughts so well that it actually causes the reader to more deeply and readily suspend disbelief, effectively rendering him a character himself, an eavesdropper, in the story.

To write realistic dialogue, the writer must pay particular attention to the nuances of the language, the little tics that are practically unnoticeable on a conscious level and that enable us to recognize one character over another when we have only the voice for comparison. In this text, assuming your basic knowledge of nouns, verbs, clauses, phrases, and sentence structure, we will discuss those nuances. For a thorough refresher on the parts of speech, sentence and paragraph structure, and punctuation, be sure to see the first book in the Thorough Primer series, *Punctuation for Writers* (Central Ave. Press, 2003).

Just as strong, active narrative engages the reader by involving him in the story, tying him emotionally and situationally to one or more characters, dialogue causes the reader to become an actual character in the story, albeit a surreptitious one, the eavesdropper. When two shady characters meet just after midnight near a lamp post on a foggy

London street to plan a murder, the reader is standing just around the corner in the shadows, listening intently. When siblings joyfully rib each other about placing First and Second in the livestock pavilion at the county fair, the reader is walking past the window, smiling at their jubilation. And when an ashen-faced astronaut looks into the on-board camera and says goodbye to his wife and children because he's just realized his spacecraft is about to explode, the reader is standing behind a mission specialist at NASA, listening to the crackling voice and staring aghast at the monitor.

Readers are human and, like all humans, any time they get a chance to eavesdrop on an otherwise private conversation, they will. You might be thinking *Not me!* and that's fine if that's what you want to believe. But the fact remains that if most humans happen to walk past an open apartment window through which they can overhear a conversation, especially an emotion-filled conversation, their pace will slacken just a bit. Subliminally, if not on more conscious levels, they want to remain within earshot of the conversation long enough to discover what's going on. That's all right; the human urge to eavesdrop is what gives dialogue its power to involve the reader in the story. Now let's take a look at the foundation of that power.

The Elements of Dialogue

Dialogue is much more than sentences surrounded by quotation marks; it is the written record of your characters' communication. And communication is considerably more abstract than physical, so what goes into dialogue? At its most basic, effective dialogue may be said to contain two parts narrative and one part nuance. The narrative parts are *tag lines* and *descriptive narrative*. Nuance, the use of which is discussed throughout this book, is composed of the subtleties of implication. That is, most of the time what your character says is no more important than how she says it as indicated by your use of punctuation or brief narrative bits. In this way, you weave dialogue and narrative to form the cloth that is the suspension of the reader's disbelief.

Tag Lines

Tag lines are those narrative bits composed of either the character's name or the appropriate personal pronoun and a simple intransitive verb that indicates utterance. A tag line might also sometimes include a **prepositional phrase**, such as "to himself" (an inanity, that) or "to no one in particular." In almost every case, prepositional phrases are unnecessary.

The purpose of the tag line is to let the reader know which character is speaking. Consequently, the best tag line is "he said" or "she said." Of course "[Character] said" is appropriate as well if you don't overuse the character's name, especially if you're dealing with dialogue between members of the same gender. Almost anything beyond this is excessive. It is valuable to remember that if each character in your story has his or her own voice, his or her own mannerisms, your need for tag lines will be practically nil. That having been said, you still should know what they are and how to use them.

Writers who use tag lines other than "he said" or "she said" most often are young in the craft and are trying to spice up the text. They believe, erroneously, that the repetitive "he said" construction is boring to the reader. In fact, the reader hardly notices the tag line at all; he quickly checks with a sidelong glance to determine, almost subliminally, which character is speaking and then leaps back into the story. After all, he's interested in the stuff *between* the quotation marks. If the work is well written, he's involved in the character, the scene, and the story, and he wants to skip over any brief narrative as quickly as possible so he can remain fully involved.

Even though they are narrative, when tag lines are handled correctly, they're minimally intrusive. Since they're also necessary in some instances (but definitely not every time a character speaks), you can't be completely rid of them. Concentrate your efforts, then, on how and when to use them. *Whether and where you use tag lines is up to you; whether they're necessary or intrusive is up to the reader.* Use tag lines only when they're absolutely necessary; otherwise, they're just extra text. Each of the following snippets of dialogue is accompanied by a tag line. In each case, my comment follows the example:

"Let's all go down to the beach!" Sandy said.

This tag line isn't intrusive, but neither is it necessary, as you'll learn when we discuss descriptive narrative.

"I don't know why she's always picking on me," John muttered to himself.

The prepositional phrase "to himself" on this tag line is completely unnecessary. "Muttered" implies that John's utterance was for himself alone.

Reverse Constructions

Sometimes, for some odd reason, the writer chooses to reverse the sequence of words in a tag line (i.e., from "Sandy said" to "said Sandy" or from "John muttered" to "muttered John"), a practice that serves no practical purpose and momentarily confuses the reader, as will any reverse construction (generally, putting the verb ahead of the subject). Remember, you want the reader to get through the tag line as quickly as possible so he can get back to being involved in the dialogue. *Unless your specific aim is to confuse the reader, don't use reverse constructions.*

More-Colorful Tag Lines

In addition to the bland "he said" "she said" tag lines, some writers use tag lines that are a little more colorful. Since tag lines are intended to be only peripheral notes and subordinate to the dialogue, these writers soon learn that more-colorful tag lines actually detract from the work: They divert the reader's attention from the scene or story line. In the following examples, we'll go from the bland to the excessively colorful:

"Come on now, Baby," she said. "You don't need that knife. What are you going to do with that?"
"I just can't stand it anymore!" he said. "I've had it!"

The first example isn't bad. We used standard tag lines and you (the reader in this case) probably all but skipped right over them. That's their purpose. Now let's look at another example with tag lines that are considerably more colorful. I've seen both these tag lines in actual manuscripts:

> She approached him cautiously. "Come on now," she cajoled. "You don't need that knife. What are you going to do with that?"
> He swung the knife in a wild arc. "I just can't stand it anymore!" he ejaculated. "I've had it!"

"Cajoled" and "ejaculated"? Where'd *that* come from? Now we're way over the top. This is the type of tag line novice writers might insert. In this dialogue, "exclaimed," "screamed," or "yelled" would fit as well as "ejaculated," but none of them do any more than tell the reader "Look, this guy's really chapped. See that exclamation point?" And since the reader already has seen the exclamation point, he doesn't need the superlatives.

Finally, a note regarding the use of commas and tag lines. When the tag line occurs before the sentence, or when the tag line occurs after a sentence that would normally end with a period, the tag line is *always* attached to the sentence with a comma:

> "I just can't go down there," he said.
> When I turned and asked him why he wasn't climbing down the rope, he said, "I just can't go down there."

Of course, when the tag line occurs at the end of a sentence that ends with a question mark or an exclamation point, there is no comma, but neither is the first word of the tag line capitalized (unless it's someone's name or another proper noun, of course). So all of the following examples are correct:

> "Let's all go down to the beach!" Sandy said.

> "Can we go down to the beach?" Sandy asked.

"Let's all go down to the beach!" she said.

"Can we go down to the beach?" she asked.

A question or an exclamation seldom needs a tag line at all. Most of the time, the earlier context of the dialogue will give the reader a sense of who is asking a question or making an exclamation. Besides, the question or exclamation itself will be indicated with a question mark or an exclamation point, so why be redundant by adding an unnecessary "she asked" or "he exclaimed"? When you do, you're telling the reader something he already knows, and that's an intrusion, albeit a very brief one, that both he and you can do without.

As you probably can see, "more colorful" isn't always a good thing. More-colorful tag lines, rather than benefiting dialogue, actually detract from the reading experience by distracting the reader and pulling him from the story line.

Brief Descriptive Narrative Passages

Because they are brief and unobtrusive, descriptive narrative passages sometimes are confused with tag lines. But whereas tag lines are limited in their use and roughly less interesting than dirt, you can convey a world of engaging information with descriptive narrative passages. For example, you can set a scene, subliminally hint at the various traits and quirks of a character, indicate the mood of the moment or of a character, and foreshadow events so quietly that the reader will believe you are a genius. Oh, and you can also use them to indicate which character is speaking. Use descriptive narrative passages to trim the "he said" "she said" fat from your manuscript.

So do we really need tag lines? After all, what do they offer other than letting us know which character is speaking? The answer is Yes, we still need them occasionally. Sometimes we don't want to convey more information than who is speaking to whom. The brief descriptive narrative passage is just one more tool, albeit a very important one, in your writer's tool box.

In the previous section, you saw the various extremes of tag lines. Now, to ease the transition from tag lines to brief descriptive narratives, let's take a look at an example with both:

> She approached him cautiously. "Come on now, Baby," she cooed. "You don't need that knife. What are you going to do with that?"
> He swung the knife in a wild arc. "I just can't stand it anymore!" he exclaimed. "I've had it!"

Notice that these tag lines are neither overpowering nor obnoxious, yet they somehow seem a bit over the top. As I mentioned earlier, much in good dialogue is implied or suggested. The introductory descriptive narrative in the same example uses two words, "approached" and "cautiously," to establish the mood of the dialogue that follows, so "cooed" isn't necessary. It might even be a bit too soft for the situation. Notice also that the first sentence of the dialogue is quiet and unassuming: "Come on now, Baby." Some of you probably are asking *But how do we know the reader will interpret that first sentence as quiet and unassuming?* Fair enough. If you hear a female character (or any character) in this situation saying "come on now" in your mind's ear, is it a harsh sound or a quiet sound? It probably is a quiet sound, especially after the reader has seen "approached" and "cautiously," two very soft words, in the narrative. Of course, you can never be certain how your reader will interpret the sounds, words, or sentences — the connotation — in your dialogue, but if it sounds true to you, it will sound true to most of your readers as well.

Let's see the same scene without tag lines at all, but with a brief introductory descriptive narrative:

> She approached him cautiously. "Come on now, Baby. You don't need that knife. What are you going to do with that?"
> "I just can't stand it anymore! I've had it!"

Does the **introductory narrative** help you see the scene a little more clearly? We know who's speaking, and we know she's approaching (and speaking) cautiously. We can almost hear her voice. Now let's try it with an additional line of narrative, but still without tag lines:

> She approached him cautiously. "Come on now. You don't need that knife. What are you going to do with that?"
> He swung the knife in a wild arc. "I just can't stand it anymore! I've had it!"

Is the scene a little more complete now, or more vivid? And does the absence of tag lines harm your (the reader's) understanding of what's going on in the scene? Of who's talking to whom?

Here are a few more examples, with and without tag lines:

> Sandy looked up and smiled. "Let's all go down to the beach!"

This brief introductory narrative not only lets the reader know who's about to speak, but lets him "see" her. It also sets the mood of the character and the scene. Did Sandy sound forced? Sorrowful? Upbeat? How she sounded to you is a subliminal effect of the introductory narrative.

> John kicked at a soda can lying alongside the curb. "I don't know why she's always picking on me," he muttered.

In this example, we've added a brief introductory narrative and kept the tag line. Although the introductory narrative sets the mood for the line of dialogue, retaining the tag line with the verb "muttered" indicates that John spoke quietly and probably bitterly. To indicate the mood and the tone of his voice (and to imply that he's alone), we might use a different introductory narrative:

John turned away from the group, kicking at a soda can lying alongside the curb. "I don't know why she's always picking on me."

By writing that John "turned away," we've implied that he has separated himself and is more or less alone. This turning away, combined with kicking at a can, also indicates his mood and implies that his voice is quiet.

Joanna sidled up alongside Tommy. "Are we going to the beach today?"

Does the introductory narrative leading in to this line of dialogue set the scene at all? Does it give us any idea of the relationship that exists between Joanna and Tommy, for example? Does it give us a sense of Joanna's voice or mood?

Joanna sidled up alongside Tommy, one finger twirling a strand of her hair. "Are we going to the beach today?"

How about now? Is this more detailed narrative better? More informative? Now take a look at the final two examples for this section:

Joanna smiled. "Are we going to the beach today?"

Joanna frowned. "Are we going to the beach today?"

As you can see, it isn't always the dialogue itself that sets the mood. Brief descriptive narrative passages can make all the difference. How does Joanna's voice sound in the first example? How does it sound in the last example?

A few more examples that are a little more in-depth follow:

John was bent over his workbench, studying a pair of lenses when Mary walked in. "Almost finished there?" she asked.
"Hi, Sweetheart. I should be done in . . . oh, a half-hour or so. What are you — Oh man! I forgot!" he exclaimed.

As before, the tag lines don't seem overly intrusive, but read the following example, then decide which is better:

> John was bent over his workbench, studying a pair of lenses when Mary walked in. "Almost finished there?"
> "Hi, Sweetheart. I should be done in . . . oh, a half-hour or so. What are you — Oh man! I forgot!"

Obviously, from the examples above we don't know what's going to happen next in this scene. If you'd rather let the reader off the hook and give him some notion of whether John and Mary will enjoy a peaceful evening or end up throwing things at each other, add a touch of color to the introductory narrative:

> John was bent over his workbench, studying a pair of lenses when Mary walked in. An impish smile creased her lips. "Almost finished there?"
> "Hi, Sweetheart. I should be done in . . . oh, a half-hour or so. What are you — Oh man! I forgot!"

Now we can be relatively sure Mary was more entertained than annoyed by John's oversight, whatever it was.

Brief Interruptive Narrative Passages

Up to this point, we've discussed *introductory* descriptive narrative passages, but you can also insert brief narrative passages between lines of dialogue. The occasional interruption helps the rhythm of the dialogue and indicates action as the character speaks. After all, characters don't simply remain static while they deliver a line of dialogue. The scene that follows is excerpted from my short story, "Mama's Taste in Men." Notice the action narrative used both to introduce and to interrupt dialogue, providing a sense of ongoing action while the characters speak:

When Joe Ray said what he said I just kind of went nuts for a minute. I shoved him hard and he stumbled backward, tripping over a half-eaten bale of hay and landing squarely between old Josie-cow's front legs. The commotion hardly bothered her at all. As I hovered over Joe Ray with my fists raised, Josie took her next mouthful of hay from between his legs. "Dang it, Joe Ray! You take that back!"

Shooting his hands down to form a cup and ward off what he was sure would be an agonizing death by cow-bite, Joe Ray sounded on the verge of tears. In fact, he was almost shrieking. "I didn't *mean* nothing, Vernon! You *know* I didn't mean nothing! Get her away from me.'"

Lester and Sam Broden leaned hard against Josie's shoulders, trying to push her back, but they were laughing too hard to have much effect. She did back up though, but not before a big string of cow slobber anchored itself just above Joe Ray's coveralls and stretched up along the right side of his neck and face. Lester and Sam lost it completely then, and collapsed on the ground alongside Joe Ray. It was all I could do not to join them, even in the gravity of the moment, even though Joe Ray had just slandered my mother. I did laugh a little, but I kept frowning too, just in case Joe Ray looked up.

The collapse of the Broden twins had convinced Josie to feed elsewhere, and she snorted and turned away, plodding around the corner of the barn with nary a backward glance. My fist relaxed and I reached for Joe Ray's hand. "Mean it or not, you shouldn't say bad things about my mama."

He took my hand and I helped him to his feet. "I just said she had bad taste in men," he said, wiping cow spit off his face with one hand and dusting off his coveralls with his hat. "Besides, it was only a joke."

"Well, some things you just don't joke about. Besides, that ain't exactly what you said. You said if Mama's taste for men was in her mouth, her breath would smell like dung."

"That was the joke part."

"Well, in the future, keep your stupid sense of humor to yourself." I thumped his chest with my forefinger. "Else you could wind up covered with cow slobber. Besides, Jake's okay. He just don't have any nose holes."

"Nostrils."

"What?"

Sam spoke up. "Nostrils. Nose holes are called nostrils."

"How do you know?"

Lester, who generally *knows* what everybody knows, put in his two cents. "*Everybody* knows that, Vernon. Nostrils is short for nose holes."

I snorted. "That's the dumbest thing I ever heard."

"Maybe dumb and maybe not so dumb, but it's true all the same." Lester was tired of arguing, so Sam closed in for the kill. The Broden Brothers Tag Team.

"We'll wait 'til school and ask Miss Durb. She knows all about such things."

That was my cue to end it. "Fine. We'll ask Miss Durb. But school ain't 'til Monday and Mama's wedding is tomorrow. So we're on truce 'til Monday." I stuck out my hand, palm down, offering them the sign of the truce. "Agreed?"

You will have noticed that not all of the narrative passages, either introductory or interruptive, in the excerpt were brief. As you study the excerpt, you'll also find that the passages are active and do not convey anything that I could have conveyed better through dialogue.

The Subtleties of Implication

The subtleties of implication are the atoms that make up the molecules of nuance. Implication, hinting at something through your use of punctuation and brief narrative bits rather than saying it directly, is one of the most powerful tools at a writer's disposal for luring the reader into the story line. When we tell the reader everything, he is knowledgeable, but passive and bored. But when we hint at certain things and allow the reader to figure it out for himself, he becomes an active participant in the story. Implication allows the reader to fill in the details that make the story more real, and it provides clues that will keep him involved.

The Physical Nuances

One of the most often used and least often thought-of nuances is physical: the use of quotation marks to indicate spoken thought. When the reader sees a set of quotation marks, he assumes subliminally that the words within them comprise a character's spoken thoughts. For this reason, it is important that we not set unspoken thoughts in quotation marks. Few things are more annoying for the reader than to read something like the following:

> "How am I ever going to get us out of this mess?" John thought.

When you first began reading the example, didn't you fully expect to find "John said" or "John asked" or some other indicator that John was speaking aloud? But instead, you saw "John thought." You can see how this sort of thing can be disconcerting for a reader. And in this case, I actually warned you it was coming. The reader has no such warning when the writer suddenly slaps a character's unspoken thoughts inside a brace of quotation marks.

To indicate spoken thought (dialogue), use quotation marks. To indicate unspoken thought, use italics. Take a look at the examples below, each of which is accompanied by a brief introductory narrative passage:

> John rubbed his chin. "How am I ever going to get us out of this mess?"

> John rubbed his chin. *How am I ever going to get us out of this mess?*

The difference is amazing, isn't it? Notice that we didn't use a tag line ("John said" or "John thought") at all, yet you know which time he was speaking aloud and which time he was thinking.

For a more in-depth discussion of the physical nuances, see "The Importance of Punctuation in Dialogue" in Chapter 2.

The Abstract Nuances

I've used abstract nuances of the language in almost every example in this book. For example, earlier I used this example to illustrate the value of brief introductory narrative:

> Joanna sidled up alongside Tommy. "Are we going to the beach today?"

Do you see that *sidled* indicates a certain mood? Now study the following similar examples:

> Joanna ran up alongside Tommy. "Are we going to the beach today?"

> Joanna stomped up alongside Tommy. "Are we going to the beach today?"

> Joanna plodded up alongside Tommy. "Are we going to the beach today?"

> Joanna walked up alongside Tommy. "Are we going to the beach today?"

Does the mood of the sentence or character change when we replace the action verb? Does Joanna's tone of voice change?

In the examples above, although we get a changing picture of Joanna's actions, mood, and voice, we are given no clues regarding the relationship between Joanna and Tommy. He could be her boyfriend, her brother, or just a friend. Because the verb, in every case, indicates that she seems to know him, we assume he isn't a stranger, and because the narrator uses his first name, we assume he isn't her father or uncle. Let's provide the reader with a stronger hint about the relationship between the characters:

> Joanna sidled up alongside Tommy, one finger twirling a strand of her hair. "Are we going to the beach today?"

Are we pretty sure Joanna and Tommy are not siblings now? (Of course, much depends on the ages of the characters and so on. A three year-old little sister might well twirl her hair as she talks with her four or five year-old brother.) As you can see, implication is a powerful part of the storytelling experience.

To include further examples here would be a duplication of effort. Please look for the nuances of implication, both physical and abstract, in the other examples in this book and in all your reading.

Sentences Versus Sentence Fragments

Despite what your English 101 professor told you, it isn't always best to write in grammatically complete sentences. Very few human beings speak in complete, correct sentences, and you should ban your characters from doing so unless one of them happens to be a particularly strict grammarian.

Earlier I mentioned that implication (or suggestion) is one of the more powerful tools at a writer's disposal for luring the reader into the story line. Writing dialogue in fragments rather than whole sentences is chief among the tricks of implication. Just as a whisper will cause a listener to lean forward in her chair and pay closer attention, so will an incomplete sentence cause the reader to lean further into the book and pay closer attention. And besides, dialogue written in sentence fragments presents the spontaneity and free-flowing rhythms of everyday speech. In other words, it's more realistic.

The most common sentence fragment is the command composed of a verb with *you* as the implied subject. For example, when a mother sees her young son racing across her unfenced yard toward the street and on an intercept course with a speeding vehicle, she isn't going to take the time to say "Johnny, stop." Instead, she'll simply yell, "Stop!" Now, every sentence has a subject and a verb; in this case the verb is *stop* and the subject is the implied *you* (*you* being the person to whom the first character is speaking, in this case, Johnny). So the one-word command isn't really a sentence fragment at all. It has a verb, which is seen, and a subject, which is implied. But for our purposes, we'll consider the one-word command a sentence fragment.

Other fragments are words, phrases, or dependent clauses that probably would not make sense outside the context of the dialogue. What does the following dependent clause mean to you?

"Just after it stopped raining."

Probably not much. Does it make more sense when presented in the context of a dialogue?

"Hey John, what time did you leave the party last night?"
"Why?"
"Just wondering."
"Just after it stopped raining."

In the above example, the only complete sentence is the first one. In each of the others, the thought is complete (through implication or suggestion) but not grammatically correct. A grammatically correct, stilted version of the same conversation might go something like this:

"Hey John, what time did you leave the party last night?"
"Why do you want to know what time I left the party?"
"I was just wondering."
"I left just after it stopped raining."

Too many complete, grammatically correct sentences in dialogue render it linear, stilted, and boring. Of course, that isn't to say you can't write a story in which a particular character speaks only in complete sentences, choosing and enunciating each word carefully. But most people (and characters) don't talk like that.

Remember that your characters are familiar with each other, just as you are familiar with your friends and family members and acquaintances. Remember, too, that your characters (and the reader) understand the context of the dialogue, just as you understand the context of the dialogue when you speak with someone. When you allow your characters to conduct their dialogue in fragments (like a real conversation), it makes the reader feel a more accepted, intimate part of the story.

Dialogue Across the Genres

During the course of my writing this book, a friend asked *Does dialogue differ among the genres? SF versus romance for example?*

The short answer is No. Each genre certainly has its own vocabulary, but the way the vocabulary is used in dialogue (or in narrative, for that matter) to provide information doesn't change.

Dialect

This section could as easily have been included in Chapter 4, "How to Lose a Reader," but dialect isn't really a story stopper unless it's done poorly. Unfortunately, writers almost always go overboard in their attempt to indicate dialect with **truncated** words, and almost every time **phonetic spelling** is used to indicate dialect, it is overused. The rule of thumb is this: If it's difficult for you to keep up with your own truncated and phonetic spellings to make sure they're consistent, don't use them. After all, if the reader is paying more attention to the individual bits of dialect (most often because he's trying to decipher them), the writer has defeated her purpose.

Sticks and Stones . . .
may break my bones, but words . . . ummm . . . nope, seems words will break my bones too.

The use of dialect goes directly to the heart of characterization, so I should remind you that all characters, initially, are *types* with whom the reader can immediately identify. We identify them as types by the assignment of general, stereotypical character traits — that is, character traits that are widely accepted as factual by the public despite their accuracy. After we establish the characters' general type, we give our main characters (usually at least the **protagonist** and **antagonist**) additional, unique traits and quirks that further identify them as individuals who, like all individuals, are more than just types.

With that said, remember this: *When you indicate the dialect of a character, you will evoke a particular* **stereotype***, whether by gender, race, geography, or some other factor.* Even if you immediately add the unique traits and quirks that render the character much more than a stereotype, some readers won't get that far with you. They'll be on the phone, talking to their lawyer about drawing up a lawsuit against you for gender bias or racial inequity or geographical indifference or picking your nose in public or . . . well, you get the idea.

The whole thing puts me in mind of my youth, when either I or my sister, riding in the back seat of my dad's '57 Chevy, might suddenly cry out, *"Mom! He's looking at me!"* or *"Mom! She's touching me!"* or *"Mom, s/he called me a jerk!"* Most of us eventually realized that what others think of us doesn't change who we really are. We lucky ones grew out of such oversensitive, self-indulgent personalities, but apparently not all of us did.

In this unfortunate age, your right to free speech has been all but usurped by everyone else's right to censor any speech that "offends" them — not simply the right to quit listening, but to make you quit speaking! When you refuse to lie or spout the party line rather than utter an unpopular or politically incorrect opinion, when society attaches ultimate importance to the reader's perception and thereby all but invalidates your authorial intent, you're liable to catch some serious heat if you strike someone the wrong way, even if what you write is the truth. My point is this: If you aren't willing to take that heat, you should consider avoiding writing dialect altogether. That having been said, if you're still interested in testing the mine field, read on.

Truncated Words and Phonetic Spelling

Truncated words are those the writer cuts short to create a particular effect in the reader. An apostrophe commonly takes the place of the missing letters. Most common among truncated words used to indicate dialect are gerunds in which the "g" has been replaced with an apostrophe, such as "goin'," "feelin'," and so on. Others include words like "gov'ment" or "s'pose" in which an entire syllable has been replaced with an apostrophe.

Trying to indicate the dialect of a particular character or group of characters is tricky at best, not only because of the aforementioned political correctness but because it is labor intensive. For example, if you use a truncated word to indicate dialect, you have to use the same apostrophe in the same place in the same word for the same character every time. And if a character says "goin'" instead of "going," that's fine, but he has to say "goin'" almost every time as well. I say *almost every time* because a character doesn't speak exactly the same way in every situation. Teenager Character might say to Mother Character, "I'll be right back. I'm goin' over to Donny's house." On the other hand, it's difficult to say "goin' to" so in another situation he might use "gonna" instead: "Why are you always on me about picking up my room? I said I was gonna do it." And if Mother Character berates him just a little, he might say, "I'm *going* to, Mom! Right now!" this time fully pronouncing the "ing" of "going" because of the emphasis he puts on the word. Can you see this one teenage character using the three different forms of "going" in the different situations? And if you use truncated words to indicate dialect, you have to think your way through every instance to be sure you're using the right form in the right situation. Might be easier to just using "going" in every case and let the reader apply his own dialect to the character. Of course, if you have several characters, some of whom say "goin'" and some of whom say "going," well, you can see what I mean when I say using truncated spellings is "labor intensive." Can you think of some real-life examples of one or more people who change the pronunciation of a word according to the circumstances?

How about phonetic spelling and irregular contractions, like that "gonna" thing we just talked about? Using phonetic spelling to indicate dialect is a little less tricky and a little less labor intensive. The trick here is to use the more common phonetic spellings and irregular contractions, those that directly mimic the sound of human speech, such as "gonna" or "would've" (not "would of") or "could've" (not "could of") and so on.

Most importantly, to write dialect that actually complements your story line instead of hindering it, you have to trust your reader. In other words, don't overdo it. When it comes to using truncated or phonetic spelling to indicate dialect, less is more. It's also important to remember that any language affectation meant to indicate dialect should be used only when it is essential that the reader recognizes a certain character type. For example, if you're writing a story set in the deep south, do you necessarily need to use truncation or phonetic spellings to indicate dialect? Probably not. You probably can trust that your reader has some sense of the sounds of language when it's spoken in the south. By the same token, if a story in set in Boston, you can "Park your car before the bar and have a beer" and trust the reader to provide the dialect. Or, if you'd rather, you can forge ahead and tackle the nightmare (and pass it on to your reader) of having to try to write the dialect itself: "Pahk youa cah befoah thu bah an' have a beah." How long would you continue to read a book full of sentences like that one? Yuck.

38

The following excerpt from "Jonas Unloads," an essay or vignette, depending on which editor you ask, is an example of a good use of dialect and phonetic spelling:

Jonas shoved the newspaper across the kitchen table and narrowly avoided knocking over the dominos. "Did you see this here crap in the newspaper? I used to think I *knew* the gov'ment, but I sho' don' know *these* guys. Where they get off tellin' me I got to support somebody I don' even know? I thought they was gonna *stop* all that crap! Where they get off tellin' me people who don' even *wanna* work got more rights than I got? An' here I am, done been workin' hard since I was six. Lord! That's been sixty-some years! An' now they wantin' me to pay more to keep it goin'! I swear, it's enough to make a man go Republican!"

"Calm down, Jonas. They just sayin' we all got to help our fellow citizens who's down on they luck, that's all."

"Nah, that *ain't* all either. Look here, Clement — supposin' they put this plan of theirs into motion an' they start makin' you an' me work harder to pay other folks' way. If they ain't gonna end it now, or even calm it down some, where's it s'pose to end?"

"We ain't gonna pay nobody's way, Man. We just gonna help 'em awhile — you know, 'til they gets on they feet again. Then they pay they *own* way, *an' then* they helps you an' me get somebody *else* on they feet. See? Nobody got no more rights than nobody else. Ever'body helps ever'body else."

"Okay, so if I wrecks my car on my way home tonight, you an' some other people gonna get me another car? An' if I gets hurt in that wreck, you gonna pay my doctor bills? I bet not!"

"Oh, come on, Jonas. You got you own money — you can pay for all that stuff you'self. But if you was down on you luck an' did'n *have* no money, then that'd be right. Then we'd pay all that stuff for you. Don' you care about nobody besides you'self? You oughta share what you got!"

"I got my *own* money? You mean I *make my own livin'*! I tell you what, Mr. Holier'n Me, Mr. Bleedin' Heart with a Perfect Plan. . . .

You'll notice that, although I used several truncated spellings (such as "gov'ment" and "sho' don'") and phonetic spellings (such as "gonna"), I conveyed most of the sense of dialect through whole words and phrases used in different ways (such as "this here crap," "They just sayin'" instead of "They're just sayin'," and "You got you own money" instead of "You've got your own money").

When you're fairly certain your reader will be able to "hear" a character's voice because it's widely known, you can create dialect simply by introducing a stereotype, manufacturing a context, and using a few terms that fit that type. Here's an example, excerpted from a brief political satire I wrote some years ago about President Clinton. In this scene, he's told me he's going to run for an unprecedented third term:

> "Would that be immediately after you pull the troops out of Bosnia?"
> He leaned forward. "What's that?"
> "Bosnia. You sent troops to Bosnia, and you told the American people they'd be home in time for Christmas, 1996. Just before the last election. If you run again, do you suppose you might actually bring them home in time to vote for you, say by November, 2000?"
> He sat back and smiled. "Oh, the *troops*. I knew there was something I'd forgotten. Sure, sure. I'll bring them back before then." His voice took on a more serious tone as he clenched his bottom lip between his teeth. "Anyway, Billy Bob Joe Ray Don DePew of Lone Skunk, Arkansas — a buddy of mine and sort of the patron saint of Arkansas governors and presidents — came up with a real good idea: we guarantee the vote of the little people by suppressing them, and at the same time we make them *think* we're taking care of them." He slapped the desk and laughed. "Ain't that just the mule's behind?"
> I smiled politely and tried to hide my incredulity. "How can you do that?"

In this excerpt, the phrase "Billy Bob Joe Ray Don DePew of Lone Skunk, Arkansas" instills not only a type but a caricature of a type — a stereotype — in the reader's mind. The president's use of words and phrases such as "buddy," "sort of," and "real good idea" furthers the sense of type and the attending dialect. His slapping the desk and his utterance of "Ain't that just the mule's behind?" cements the deal.

Finally, the following excerpt from my short story, "Soft as a Breeze," is quasi-dialogue; that is, it's narrative, but directed at the reader as if he were a character in the story. See whether you can spot the nuances that make the voice of this character different from the voices of the characters in the two previous excerpts:

> . . . we still watched him like he was our kid or somethin'. I mean we *always* watched, like it was just a regular thing we did. Not like we had to think about it. Like somethin' you have to do but you don't mind 'cause it's just what you always do, natural like.
>
> Anyway, I was tryin' to make out what Mick was braggin' about when that hole broke. That's when Jimmy became the Digger. The guys said he never said nothin'. Didn't jump or scare or nothin', just ran, soft and easy like, glided, like, to the hole and started right in diggin'. Then everybody else jumped and stumbled and cussed and fell all over each other tryin' to help him dig.
>
> They all dug, I guess, even the lieutenant, for most of an hour, 'cept the louie told me later it was only a few minutes. But nobody dug like Jimmy. And they said he never said a word and never stopped. Just kept on diggin', soft like, 'til he found my boot. Then he yelled *Hey!* they said, but never stopped diggin' even then, not even for a second. Just tore in a little quicker, I guess. Still soft-like, you know, but not quite as soft.
>
> Anyway, somebody said it was Mick that tugged on my boot, but he sure didn't tug like he talked. If he'd tugged like he talked he'd have tugged hard, hopin' just the boot and my foot or leg

would come out. But he just gave a little tug, like he hoped it wasn't loose but still attached. 'Course the boot *didn't* come out alone, neither. It never came off 'til I took it off myself, later.

Do you see the differences in nuance between the voice in this excerpt and the ones that went before? This character, like any major character, has a certain speech pattern. Look for repeated words and phrases that seem his favorites. They are what differentiate this character's voice from the voices of the characters in the previous excerpts.

A Note on the Mechanics of Punctuation in Dialogue

As I mentioned earlier, *Punctuation for Writers* is a definitive look at how the writer can use punctuation and grammar based on the effect you want to evoke in your reader rather than on some arbitrary rules. For your convenience, in Chapter 2 of this book I also provide a brief refresher on punctuation, as an introduction to my discussion of using punctuation to inject emotion into dialogue. Although that discussion is fairly thorough, I thought it best to discuss the strictly mechanical uses of punctuation here.

The Use of Single and Double Quotation Marks

Use quotation marks (double quotation marks) to indicate spoken thought. **End punctuation** is enclosed within the quotation marks. You can see this at work in every example of dialogue in this book.

Use single quotation marks (looks like an apostrophe) to indicate that one character is directly quoting another character:

> "So after the first couple beers, we were getting pretty loose. I said to Sandy, 'Think you'd like to go out some time?' And she says, 'I'd love to, but not with you.' Can you believe the nerve?"

In the above example, notice that the character is quoting precisely what he said to Sandy and her response. Notice that the first letter of each imbedded (directly quoted) sentence is capitalized and that each imbedded sentence has its own end punctuation. Notice too that all the end punctuation is enclosed within both the single and double quotation marks. Many writers dodge this problem by simply having characters paraphrase other characters:

> "So after the first couple beers, we were getting pretty loose. I asked Sandy whether she'd like to go out some time, and she actually said she would, but not with me. Can you believe the nerve?"

Of course, you can also elect to go with a partial quotation to place emphasis on that part of the sentence:

> "So after the first couple beers, we were getting pretty loose. I asked Sandy whether she'd like to go out some time, and she actually said, 'I'd love to, but not with you.' Can you believe the nerve?"

A caution – do not use quotation marks, single or double, to indicate unspoken dialogue (thought). Instead, use italics.

Paragraphing Dialogue

The indentation is not a mark of punctuation, obviously, but it might as well be. When writing dialogue, it is important to remember to begin a new paragraph (indent) every time a different character begins to speak or each time the narrative shifts to a different character. The indentation at the beginning of a new paragraph tells the reader subliminally that the point of view has changed from the narrator to a character, from one character to another, or from a character to the narrator.

In the first snippet of dialogue that follows, there is no narrative, not even a tag line. Notice the use of indentation to indicate the beginning of a new paragraph each time a different character begins to speak:

"John, what's going on? I heard you were hanging out with Deb Fossey yesterday, that maybe you guys took in a movie or something. What's up with that?"

"Yeah, *A River Runs Through It*. Not a bad flick."

"You know that's not what I meant. Last I heard, you thought she was a total flake."

The next example shows the same technique when dialogue is combined with brief introductory narrative passages. For the sake of comparison, the dialogue is changed only minimally:

Nick grinned broadly, slapping John on the back as he caught up with him. "So what's going on? I heard you were hanging out with Deb Fossey yesterday, that maybe you guys took in a movie or something. What's up with that?"

In the middle of his morning run, John slackened his pace only momentarily. "*Yeah, A River Runs Through It.*" He glanced at Nick and smiled. "Not a bad flick."

"Ha ha! You know that's not what I meant. Last I heard, you thought she was a total flake."

A Note on Overuse

Many writers, especially those who are relatively new to the craft, tend to overuse the question mark and the exclamation point. Just as an ellipsis isn't rendered any more effective by adding extra periods, neither is a question mark or exclamation point made more effective through repetition. In every case, use only one question mark or exclamation point per occurrence. The ellipsis consists of three periods, with a space before and after each. When the ellipsis occurs at the end of a sentence, it is followed by the appropriate end punctuation, whether a period, a question mark, or whatever. When the end punctuation is a period, it looks as if the ellipsis is formed of four spaced periods, but that is not the case.

Summary

Writing realistic dialogue is a constant balancing act between providing the reader with enough information so he isn't confused and not providing so much that he pays more attention to the nuances than to the dialogue itself. You provide that information through the dialogue itself, tag lines, brief introductory or **interruptive narrative** passages, implication, and sometimes dialect. It isn't easy, but hearing the first person who is neither family member, friend, nor acquaintance raving about the dialogue in your book makes the struggle worthwhile.

Chapter 2   Conveying Emotion

Just as music has been defined as that which occurs between the notes, many writers believe the story is that which occurs between the lines of dialogue. The emotion-laden lines of dialogue are the ones we remember from our favorite films, plays, and books. Emotion-filled dialogue not only reveals the character of the players and conveys their emotions, but enables the reader to experience the same emotions. The following quote by my friend, Penny Porter, says it nicely:

> "Emotion-laden phrases . . . do more than just carry the story. Statements with feeling . . . make the story unforgettable . . . . The display of feelings is the single most important part of that all-important, unforgettable scene that sets the stage and involves the reader. And, if feelings can be shown through emotion-laden dialogue, such as "Do something, Daddy!" when the barn is burning down, that's all you need to hook your reader — then it's just a matter of keeping a promise, living up to your dialogue."

In this chapter, we'll discuss the nuances of providing emotion through dialogue and its attendant narrative. You'll learn to reveal through dialogue the traits, good and bad, of your characters. You'll learn that the connotation, the implication, of a word is almost always more important than the denotation. And we'll break it down further than that. You'll learn how to use specific letters, words, and punctuation to cause your reader to experience your characters' emotions by causing her to speed or plod through your text. You'll learn to use particular sentence and paragraph constructions to excite or lull your reader or even evoke a strong sense of drama. In short, you'll learn to create "that unforgettable scene that sets the stage and involves the reader." Let's get started.

The Elusive Traits of Realistic Dialogue

Some writing instructors insist on offering an array of methods or formulae that they label the *traits* or *techniques* or *special techniques* or *advanced techniques* of dialogue. Fooey. The purpose of dialogue, by way of conveying the thoughts of the characters to the reader, is to draw the reader into your world for the duration of your story or essay or novel.

The only way to draw the reader into your work and keep him there is to suspend his disbelief, his sense of reality. I know most of you are fictionists — a term I coined to include those who write novels, novellas, shorts stories, vignettes, screenplays, plays, and political speeches — and that there's a sprinkling of essayists out there as well. But even a newspaper item must grab a reader's interest, must pull her from her world for a few minutes, if the author expects to someday take over the city desk. And as a former college instructor, I can tell you that although I had to read all the term papers in order to grade them, I often read the interesting ones more than once. If this concept applies to newspaper articles and term papers, how much more strongly must it apply to creative writing?

If your purpose is to draw your reader into your world for the duration, everything you put on the page — every word, every sentence, and every bit of punctuation — must be placed with a thought for how it will affect the reader. All other considerations are secondary. Can you do that? Yes. Do you have to work at it, or is it automatic? Again, yes. You have to work at it at first, but as you become more familiar with using the nuances of language to achieve a particular effect in the reader, it will become much easier.

So far, I've talked mostly in abstracts. Let's get down to the concrete. Realistic dialogue should convey a strong sense of emotion — to that end, it should have the spontaneity and free-flowing rhythms of everyday speech — and it should enable the reader to differentiate one character from another based strictly on the character's voice.

Emotion

Realistic dialogue should be emotion laden. The most important use of dialogue is to convey the emotions of the character(s) in such a way that the reader assumes the same emotions to a similar degree. We will explore this topic in depth shortly.

Spontaneity

In every case, dialogue should have the spontaneity and free-flowing rhythms of everyday speech. In fact, it should sound exactly like real dialogue, except without the boring, mundane parts (unless the character is boring and mundane in the story). Spontaneous dialogue also is engaging and memorable, and it will pull your reader more deeply and more quickly into the story line.

One of the easiest, quickest ways to ensure spontaneity is through the use of contractions. Very few people talk without using contractions. If one of your characters speaks very carefully and very succinctly, she might not use contractions at all, but even in a room full of English teachers, she will be the exception, not the rule. You can also use contractions to subliminally differentiate one character from another. For example, one character might habitually say "can't," another "cannot," and a third — should you decide to play with dialect a bit — "cain't."

If you want a practical exercise in learning to write spontaneous, realistic dialogue, visit your local chain restaurant between, say, midnight and three in the morning two or three times a week for a few weeks. Make sure you mix-in a Monday night (the night after the first day of work for most people), a Friday night and a Saturday night (the two nights when most people don't have work obligations the next day), a Sunday night (both post-religious observance and pre-work week), and one regular weeknight to provide balance and perspective.

Why an all-night restaurant? Because there, and during those hours, you'll witness a microcosm of society: cops, laborers, lawyers, drunks, doctors, politicians, hookers, dealers, and poets will come and go, sometimes together. Take along a small notebook and a pen or pencil. Then sit back and, as inconspicuously as possible, write what you hear. Write the dialogue that you overhear and take copious notes on the people and situations around you. As often as not, and usually without you realizing it until after the fact, the dialogue will turn up in one of your characters, the people will become characters, and the situations will become story lines.

Character Identification

There's no better way to ensure realistic dialogue than to let your characters speak the way they would speak if they were actual people. Realistic dialogue will reveal (or hint at) the character's education level, the character's relationship with the other characters, and the character's reaction to her surroundings. Perhaps most importantly, in our current society, if your character wouldn't curse on a dare, don't make her curse, but if your character happens to be that inner-city gang member, don't make him talk as if he's the local banker or the church lady. Sounds simple, I know, but the eighty-two year old ranch hand will speak in a different way than will the 15 year old member of an inner-city gang. A well-educated character will speak in a different way than will the high-school dropout or the guy who's spent the first forty years of his life pursuing various doctoral degrees of philosophy. *Well-educated* and *professional student* are not necessarily synonymous.

I hope that you, as a writer, recognize that words — *all* words — are nothing more or less important than vehicles for communication. I'd never advocate setting out to intentionally offend anyone, but neither would I consider changing dialogue just to appease some oversensitive clod who's probably faking being offended anyway. I'd rather go unpublished.

If you'd rather *not* go unpublished, take a look at these suggestions for bringing your characters to life through dialogue:

Allow the character to use certain favorite words or catch phrases. On the long-running television series *Gunsmoke*, one of Festus' catch phrases was "Don'tcha see?" Mr. Burns, a grizzled, conniving old character on *The Simpsons*, occasionally mutters "Excellent!" I'm sure you can think of dozens of other examples.

Allow the character, through her dialogue, to reveal her own personality as well as the personalities of other characters. Characters can reveal how they feel about a particular situation or another character, not only with what is said and but also with what is implied:

> "You lied to me! You said you were going for a drive."
> "C'mon, Baby . . . . I didn't say I was going *alone*."

Allow your characters to interrupt each other. Among many other reasons that we'll discuss later, interruptions help establish the characters' personalities. The one who constantly interrupts might be pushy, brash, or rude; the one who constantly allows the interruption might be a doormat.

Every good salesman knows that the person who asks the questions controls the conversation. Apply that knowledge to your characters. If you want to indicate a struggle for control, one way is to allow your characters to bounce questions off each other for awhile. Of course, any struggle for control is a conflict and a way to create or intensify tension:

> "If you knew she'd be there, why did you go?"
> "What difference does it make who was there?"
> "Well, was she there or not?"
> "Jeez, can you just get off my back for five minutes?"

We know the true purpose of realistic dialogue: to draw the reader into your world for the duration. We know that to accomplish that, you don't need a bunch of stuffy methods or formulae. We know that to write well, you need only remain mindful of the reader. If you learn absolutely nothing else from this entire book, you will be immeasurably ahead of your peers if you just remember that *everything you put on the page — every word, every sentence, and every bit of punctuation — must be placed with a thought for how it will affect the reader.* All other considerations are secondary.

Keep that in mind and buckle up.

Influencing the Mood of the Reader

Now, as general rules go, here's another keeper for you: A longer sentence conveys emotion; a shorter sentence evokes a sense of drama. First of all, this isn't a theorem; it is a fact. A longer sentence *always* more easily and more readily conveys emotion, thereby tying the reader more closely to the character and story line. And a shorter sentence *always* evokes a sense of drama, thereby heightening the level of tension in the reader and engaging him, again tying him more closely to the story line. It's important to note, though, that the way the writer delivers sentences of varying lengths is as important to their overall effectiveness as the fact that she uses them at all. The following narrative sentence is excerpted from my short story, "Soft as a Breeze":

> I mean there's a big lead-up that's sort of excitin' and scary and lasts longer than time when things are happening all around you and you're diving for a hole and grabbing your rifle and trying to stick a magazine in upside down and throwing ammo to your buddy and dodging sounds all at once, kind of like a spooked house cat.

Notice that not only is the sentence long, but you probably sped up as you read further into it. If you aren't sure whether it affected you, read through it again and see whether you speed up. I'd almost bet your heart rate increased a bit too. These effects are due not only to the physical length of the sentence, but also to the lack of punctuation and the specific words used. Your reading speed and heart rate involuntarily increasing indicate that your emotional level also is on the increase. This is true of anxiety (as probably in this case), elation, love, hatred, and so on through the range of human emotions. If this sentence didn't affect you at all, that's all right. It's tame compared with many of the sentences in "Soft as a Breeze."

Reading too many long sentences in succession can confuse or tire the reader. You must take care to ensure that each word conveys precisely what you want it to convey, that it begins where you want it to begin, wends its way through the appropriate emotional buttons, and ends abruptly enough to achieve the desired effect. Often times, a longer sentence must be crafted with an eye toward setting the reader up for a shorter sentence — the dramatic punch that ties the whole thing together. A very short sentence that follows a series of longer sentences will evoke in the reader an immediate and strong sense of drama, rather like a literary punch in the gut. In this excerpt from the same short story, you'll find two long sentences, the second considerably shorter than the first, followed by a very short sentence fragment in its own paragraph:

> You start to stop shaking and you think of a cigarette and reach for one and Mom flashes a disapproving look through your mind but you reach anyway, then you want to joke with your friend, show him you're both still bad, tell him Charlie'd rather sandpaper a bear's ass in a phone booth than mess with you and he smiles kind of soft in your mind and you want to offer to split that extra beer in your pack with him, you know? *Split a beer with the wind* you think maybe help *his* nerves a little bit and you smile, so you think to reach for it but decide to joke first and get the beer in a second and you're smiling and turning your head and opening your mouth to tell him about bear's asses in phone booths —
> *But his face is gone.*

For purposes of study and argument, I'll tell you that my intent with the above example was to have the reader go quickly through a very long first sentence, then give him a minor respite with a comma and very short clause: "you know?" Following the long pause (reader's rest) provided by the question mark, I plunged him back into another long sentence, hoping the fact that he'd just finished an even longer one would cause him to speed even faster, in his impatience, through this one. Then, at the end of the second sentence and the paragraph, he hits an em dash, which is a less-sudden stop than a period (rather like a parachute on the back of a dragster), and then the dramatic punch: "But his face is gone." Right now, *you're* my reader. Did it work? If it worked for me, it can work for you.

Of course, using too many short sentences in sequence waters down the sense of drama and renders a choppy reading experience. What if the previous example had been composed of all short sentences?

> You start to stop shaking. You think of a cigarette and reach for one. Mom flashes a disapproving look through your mind, but you reach anyway. Then you want to joke with your friend. You want to show him you're both still bad. You want to tell him Charlie'd rather sandpaper a bear's ass in a phone booth than mess with you. He smiles kind of soft in your mind. You want to offer to split that extra beer in your pack with him, you know? *Split a beer with the wind,* you think. Maybe help *his* nerves a little bit. You smile. You think to reach for it, but decide to joke first and get the beer in a second. You're smiling and turning your head. You're opening your mouth to tell him about bear's asses in phone booths —
> *But his face is gone.*

Does the final sentence carry the same impact it carried before? Does the paragraph carry the same level of emotion? Of the fourteen sentences in the revised paragraph, only half are short sentences. Imagine how a paragraph full of such short sentences would dilute the impact of the final sentence.

Bear in mind that it's all right to use a series of shorter sentences if you *want* the reading experience to be choppy and tightly measured in order to cause a particular feeling or reaction in the reader. When a poet writes a dirge, chances are she'll pen a succession of short lines. If you're writing a very sad story and want to convey a measured sense of gloom or morosity, you might use a succession of short sentences.

I believe our susceptibility to the emotional or dramatic impact of longer and shorter sentences is hard-wired into the human mind. Even though few humans can consciously use a succession of shorter sentences intentionally to affect others' emotions, we all do it and we all are affected by it — though *afflicted* might be the better verb. If you think back to the last time you attended a funeral or other solemn occasion, you'll remember that those in attendance, even those speaking to each other informally, spoke in quiet, short sentences. You might explain away the quietude as a result of the hushed surroundings or even of social upbringing, but that doesn't explain the brevity of their speech.

Just as humans have little choice but to express themselves in short, choppy sentences when they experience a sad or dramatic situation, so can you instill within them, by your use of short, choppy sentences, a sense of sadness or drama. This is a significant bit of knowledge. As I mentioned earlier, although relatively few humans — mostly preachers, professional speakers, and writers — wield the power to affect emotions by manipulating sentence length, all humans are affected by it. Put another way, few are shooters, but all are targets. Now you're a shooter too.

The Sounds of Letters and Words

First, a caution: Because the concepts in the next section involve the minutiae of the sounds of the language, they require considerable explanation and examples. Some of you will require only the first explanation; others might not understand the first but will understand the second. Once you "get it," feel free to lightly scan the subsequent paragraphs until you find one that regains your interest. As I explained in the introduction to this book, I'd rather provide too many explanations and examples than too few. Let's get started.

The writer has more tools at her disposal for conveying the emotions of the characters and influencing the mood of the reader than she might imagine. Remember what I wrote earlier:

> *A longer sentence conveys emotion; a shorter sentence evokes a sense of drama.*

That thought encompasses not only the physical length of a sentence but also the speed with which a reader is transported through a word or sentence or passage by the writer's intentional use of certain letters and words in certain combinations. **Reader speed** is a function of **sound length**, the amount of time it takes to pronounce, aloud or mentally, the sound of a letter or combination of letters. For example, *B* is pronounced faster than *S* or *TH*. This measurement is constant, and it is dependent only on the relative position of the other letter(s) in the word. Because this trait is carried by the letters into words and sentences, it becomes an important tool for subliminally conveying the characters' emotions.

In fact, reader speed is a direct function not only of the individual letters and how they are combined in a word, but of the words and their juxtaposition in the sentence, the sentence itself, the use or lack of punctuation within the sentence and paragraph, and even the overall structure of the paragraph. When reader speed is on stage, sound length is backstage, feeding him lines. We won't discuss sound length in particular any further, but it will remain in the background in the upcoming discussion on the sounds of letters.

So at this juncture, we can update our initial statement: A longer sentence conveys emotion, but a longer, *faster* sentence, one that is read through quickly, conveys the emotion even more strongly. Likewise, although a shorter sentence always evokes a sense of drama, a stilted, plodding sentence can serve to instill a sense of doom or other high drama in the reader. In other words, you can manipulate the reader's mood.

We form the sounds of different letters in different ways — for example, we pronounce a B by lightly touching the lips together, almost incidentally, and then parting them as we exhale a light burst of air — we speed through some letters and words, and we are forced to plod or drag through others. We have no conscious choice. Fortunately, those letters carry that trait into the words and sentences they comprise. For example, "need" seems a longer word than "boot" and "bees" seems a longer word than "bead." More to the point since they're synonymous, "breeze" seems a longer word than "wind," and not just because it has two more letters. Both, after all, are one-syllable words. Neither is this phenomenon attributable only to the use of long vowels; the S, the soft C and others also have a softening and/or pronunciation-lengthening effect that the reader picks up on subliminally. For another example, pronouncing the SH that occurs at the beginning of some words ("ship") is a bit more difficult than pronouncing that B, and pronouncing the SH that occurs at the end of some words ("crash") mires us even further; these take a bit more time to pronounce.

To look at it in a slightly different way, we might think of S and C as *slick* letters; we pronounce them easily and quickly, especially when they're followed by a long E sound. An M at the end of a word seems to propel us into the next word, and an MS propels us even faster, especially if the next word begins with a T. The letters D and B mire us just a bit when they occur at the beginning of a word, and T, a harder consonant sound, bogs us down even more. Finally, just as an M or N at the end of a word seems to propel us into the next word, a T at the end of the word makes us struggle a bit to get there, and hitting a D at the end of a word slows us even further. Of course, encountering a TH at the end of a word is a little like walking in deep, thick mud while wearing flippers. So to extend the example I started in the previous paragraph, "seem" is more easily pronounced than "deem" or "beam" or "team;" "beat" is a little slower, "bead" is even slower, and "teeth" is the slowest among these words. Pause here for a moment and repeat these words aloud, more than once if necessary, comparing the sounds and sensing the speed.

As a general rule, the reader will read through soft consonant sounds and long vowel sounds more quickly than she will read through the other letters and sounds. Conversely, she will read through medium and hard consonant sounds and soft vowel sounds more slowly and sometimes, depending on the writer's use of punctuation and application of the rules of meter, more rhythmically.

Before we explore examples of this phenomenon, let's take a look at the sounds of some of the more commonly used letters and letter combinations. I've divided the sounds roughly into those that are pronounced with the greatest speed (soft consonants and long vowels), those pronounced a bit more slowly (medium consonants, some combinations), and those through which we virtually have to drag ourselves (hard consonants, some combinations). Of course, some sounds are pronounced faster when they occur at the beginning of a word than when they occur at the end of a word. For example, we get through the TH in *this* more quickly than we get through the TH in *truth*. As you read the following, please note that it is only a small sampling of the sounds in our language, and I mention them here only as a catalyst for your own thought process:

Some soft (faster) consonant sounds are C (like S), GH, H, S, V, W, Y, and Z.

Some medium consonant sounds are B, CL, D (when used to begin a word), F (PH), G (like J), GG, J, L, M, N, P (when used to begin a word), Q, R, SH, SL, SP, ST, and V.

Some hard (slower) consonant sounds are C (like K), CH, CK, CT, D (when used at the end of a word), DD, G, K, NCH, ND, NG, NGTH, NT, P (when used at the end of a word), PT, RD, T, TR, and TT.

The fast, hard vowel sounds are the long A, I, and E.

I'm sure you'll find other sounds that I didn't include, but that's fine. If you're thinking about the sounds of letters and how they affect words, you're well on your way to learning (sensing) another very important nuance of the language.

As I mentioned earlier, the reader will get through some words much more quickly than she'll get through others. As you saw in the excerpts from "Soft as a Breeze" above, sentences that contain faster words and that are written about an appropriate topic and with the right punctuation (or lack of punctuation) actually will cause the reader's heart rate to increase as he becomes more emotionally involved in your story line. And that's the bottom line of all this letter- and word-sound study: conveying the emotions of your characters and affecting the emotions of your reader.

The Use of Meter in Prose

Of course, since we're discussing the sounds of letters and words, I would be remiss if I failed to mention meter at least briefly. Ours is an accentual/syllabic language. Meter is the measurement of the rhythm established by the juxtaposition of accented and unaccented syllables. Meter is *not* something we can choose to impose or not impose on a piece of writing — it is always there, an integral part of the language. For example, *beneath* is a two-syllable word in which the second syllable always is more strongly accented. On the other hand, *under* is a two-syllable word in which the first syllable always is more strongly accented. If you don't believe me, try to pronounce *beneath* with the emphasis on the first syllable.

The iamb is the measure most common to the English language, and the other commonly used measures are the trochee, the dactyl, and the anapest. (The adjective forms of these words, which you also might encounter, are iambic, trochaic, anapestic, and dactylic.)

Meter	Syllable Accents	Example
iamb	weak / strong	be-NEATH
trochee	strong / weak	UN-der
dactyl	strong / weak / weak	IN-di-a / NA-po-lis
anapest	weak / weak / strong	then he FELL / to the VAL / ley be-LOW

As I mentioned earlier, meter is an integral part of our language, and not something we can choose to impose or not, but you should also know you *can* manipulate meter to achieve a particular purpose in your prose, just as you can in a poem. For example, to establish a calming, repetitive rhythm, string together a series of iambic feet. In traditional poetry, we often use five of them, which equals a line of iambic pentameter: enmeshed amidst the moon's own silv'ry rays, with the accents exaggerated, would be pronounced enMESHED aMIDST the MOON'S own SILv'ry RAYS. Each iambic foot consists of two syllables, so the division is / enMESHED / aMIDST / the MOON'S / own SIL / v'ry RAYS.

If you say this aloud, you'll be pleasantly surprised at how easily it rolls off the tongue:

enMESHED aMIDST the MOON'S own SILv'ry RAYS

Now this is a book about prose, not poetry, but bear with me. All three sound elements we've been discussing are at work in this line. The line is metered, of course, in iambic pentameter, and meter is a function of the sound and accent of syllables. But also at work in this line are several fast consonant sounds, several soft consonant sounds, and several soft vowel sounds, which serve to calm and quiet the line.

Look at the repetition of sounds in the line, and listen to them as you say the line aloud again. The N, M, NM, NS, and S are fast, slick sounds that pronounce easily and fast. The SH'D, DST, SILVRYR are cushioned, soft sounds that slow us and quiet the line. The soft E, A, and I sounds also cushion and slow the line while putting the reader or speaker at ease. Say the line aloud again. Although this is a line of iambic pentameter (verse), the techniques used here can as easily be applied to prose. Can you imagine your reader flowing through your story or essay as effortlessly as you flowed through the example?

The skillful writer, like the skillful poet, can use the hard-driving rhythm of a dactyl to cause a reader to speed up in an appropriate place, and can just as effectively use the lazy, waltzing rhythm of the anapest to cause the reader to slow down. Because of the dactyl's stressed syllable hurrying into two unstressed syllables, the reader gets the subliminal sense of speeding up or stumbling after having moved along smoothly with the usual iambic flow that will most often predominate your sentences. And the anapest's two unstressed syllables straining to reach the stressed third syllable gives the reader the sense that he's momentarily bogged down, trudging along after having moved along in that smooth iambic flow.

Make no mistake, this book is about prose, not poetry. But because poetry is more spare than prose and presents a less-muddled surface, I'll ask your indulgence for a bit longer as I use a poem to illustrate the effect that the sounds of letters and words can have on the reader. I stress, though there is a metrical structure to this poem, the sounds of the individual letters and words are even more important to the mood. I wrote "Courage, Defined in Four Acts" several years ago as an experiment in sound and meaning, to see whether I could combine the sounds of letters and words with the connotation of the context to achieve a particular effect in the reader. Please read through the entire poem so you can see the progression from hard or harsh to soft sounds. A detailed discussion follows:

Courage, Defined in Four Acts

The Cavalry

Down from the hillside, ride wild through the villages,
tracking and trampling the young ones who run;
smoke out the old ones by burning and pillaging,
stacking like cordage the dead in the sun.
Into the battle you charge with the rest of them,
screaming past courage to bludgeon your foes;
impaling their children, you bleed the will out of them,
mauling them, maiming them, onward you go.
Riding hard, rampaging, numb to the suffering
screams of the savages trampled below,
silence the screaming, your horses' hooves rumbling;
victims aren't human, the cavalry's bold.

The Bombers

Circling, zeroing in on insanity,
fly smooth and level, or they may escape.
Knowing no boundaries lessens the misery,
letting your daydreams assume nightmare shapes.
Into the battle you fly with the rest of them,
screaming past courage to bludgeon your foes,
slamming your blessings deep into the hearts of them,
mauling them, maiming them, onward you go.
Recklessly mindless and numb to the suffering
screams in the deafening thunder below,
carpet the desert with tons of steel offerings;
victims are faceless, and sanity holds.

The Fighters

Circling, zeroing in on insanity,
fly ever lower; don't let them escape!
Knowing no boundaries eases your misery;
murder the bastards; your job is their rape.
Into the battle you fly with the best of them,
screaming past courage to bludgeon your foes;
raining your rocketed blessings down onto them,
mauling them, maiming them, onward you go.
Laser-aimed armament stops all the suffering
screams in the hot conflagration below.
Silence the guns and the streets with your cannoning;
victims are faceless, and sanity holds.

The Soul

Circling, zeroing in on infinity,
soar ever higher on gossamer wings
over the boundaries into eternity;
leave all the nightmares and live in your dreams.
Into forever you soar while the rest of them
reach beyond courage to bludgeon their foes;
easing your wisdom deep into the hearts of them,
blessing them, teaching them, softly you go.
Gently and silently, seek out the reasoning
ones in the manifest mis'ry below;
whisper true courage deep into the hearts of them:
he is courageous who *withholds* the blow.

Does *The Soul* seem somehow different from the other three cantos?
How? Does your heart seem to race a bit faster while you read the first
three cantos as compared with reading the fourth? Do you feel
different emotionally while reading the first three cantos than when
you read the fourth? Let's take a closer look. The first three cantos,

which are very physical and hostile in nature, also are hostile in sound. Every line of the first canto is filled with hard sounds and, often, harsh words and images. Read the first canto again with that in mind. Try to recognize the hard sounds and harsh words. Feel free to look also for any soft sounds, especially those that last long enough to sustain a soft-sounding line. You won't find any.

Now read the second and third cantos again, paying attention to the same attributes. Notice that the first two lines of each carries considerably softer, calmer sounds. I designed this intentionally to give the reader an emotional breather before pulling him back into the depths of hatred and pain later in each stanza. "Insanity" carries a hint of harshness at the end of the first line of each stanza, but "circling, zeroing in on" is a sequence of soft to medium consonant sounds connected by soft vowels, with the less than notable exception of the long O in "zeroing." The second line of *The Bombers* is also mostly composed of soft sounds until "escape," and even it isn't harsh. The second line of *The Fighters* is a bit harsher. The lines in both cantos grow quickly and progressively harsher beginning with the third and fourth lines.

Now read the fourth canto, *The Soul*, with these same attributes in mind. You'll find very few hard sounds, and nothing harsh unless it is offered in the context of sympathy. Notice, too, the parallel structure of the cantos, the repetition. In each of the first three cantos, line 5 is similar and line 6 is identical, as is line 7. Line 8 in each of the first three cantos is especially vicious. In the final canto, though, lines 7 and 8 are particularly soft. As you did with the first canto, now look for any hard or harsh sounds or words or lines as well as soft sounds, words, and lines. You'll find that the entire stanza sustains a predominantly soft sound.

For those of you who are interested, this poem also was an experiment in determining whether dactylic tetrameter, an inherently humorous-sounding rhythm, could sustain a strong sense of drama. Because of the combination of the particularly harsh subject matter with the insistent, drumbeat-like rhythm (a dactyl or dactylic foot consists of three syllables, the first with a strong accent and the others with lesser accents), the experiment was a success.

Now let's move back to prose examples.

Remember the second excerpt we used earlier from "Soft as a Breeze," the one with two long sentences followed by one short sentence fragment? I used it to explain how sentence length could affect the reader's emotions. For ease of reference, I'll use it to explain how the sounds of letters and words can effect reader's emotions as well. While reading "Courage, Defined in Four Acts" you grew accustomed to finding the hard, stopping sounds and the consonant sounds that drag on your pronunciation of them, the ones that tend to slow you down. Look for them here:

> You start to stop shaking and you think of a cigarette and reach for one and Mom flashes a disapproving look through your mind but you reach anyway, then you want to joke with your friend, show him you're both still bad, tell him Charlie'd rather sandpaper a bear's ass in a phone booth than mess with you and he smiles kind of soft in your mind and you want to offer to split that extra beer in your pack with him, you know? *Split a beer with the wind* you think maybe help *his* nerves a little bit and you smile, so you think to reach for it but decide to joke first and get the beer in a second and you're smiling and turning your head and opening your mouth to tell him about bear's asses in phone booths —
> *But his face is gone.*

In only the first thirteen words of the first sentence ("You . . . reach"), we find these hard consonant sounds: ST'RT, T'ST'P, K'NG, 'ND, 'TH'NK, 'G'R'TT'E, and 'ND. There is only one medium consonant sound — CH — and one soft sound: SH.

The passage is composed of repeated, predominantly hard sounds, so we read through it relatively quickly. Our reader speed certainly is due in part to the lack of punctuation, but take a look at the sounds again. How smoothly does "start to stop shaking" roll off the tongue? The alliteration of the S and ST sounds helps a lot. How smoothly does "think of a cigarette" roll off the tongue (especially if you're a reformed smoker)? There are a few sticky places in the sentence, and in the second sentence, but both are predominantly very fast because they contain hard (fast) consonant sounds.

Hmmm. I mentioned smooth and sticky places in the sentence, but among her many other contributions to this work, my friend and confidant, Dawn Wink, reminded me that I failed to explain how the writer can manipulate meter in prose, especially if she is new to the idea. Basically, she asked which came first in the writing process, meter or concept. My short answer was Neither. I've been paying scrupulous attention to the nuances of the language for so long — "thinking in meter," I said — that I no longer give either much conscious thought. But I hasten to add that you will have the same ability, or curse, once you've grown accustomed to the notion that you can say what you mean *and* use the rhythms of the language. Of course, that probably doesn't help much since it's a bit like your parents telling you "someday you'll understand." But Dawn's true question was *How can I apply these techniques in my own writing?* Here's how to do it:

As a writer, you must learn two things in order to apply meter: *You must learn to read your work aloud* shamelessly, with the necessary emotion, and you must learn to trust your ear. Reading aloud will allow you to hear the rhythms of your prose. Even if you don't know anything about meter, and even if you think you can't recognize whether your prose is flowing smoothly, you will notice when you stumble or when your tongue ties itself into a knot over an awkward construction. Then the second part kicks in: *You must trust your ear*, and then work to repair the words or phrases over which you stumbled. How can you tell whether you've repaired them? Read it aloud again. And again. And again. Soon, as you begin to subliminally hear and internalize the rhythms of the language, your writing will smooth itself out as you write.

I also strongly advocate that you read others' works aloud. Sense the rhythms of their words. Will their style rub off on your own? Yes. Will it replace your own? No. None of us is completely devoid of the influence of others. As writers and poets, we fashion our writing style by absorbing and refitting and merging the styles of others.

Well, here we are again: *A longer sentence conveys emotion; a shorter sentence evokes a sense of drama.* Does our mantra have a different meaning for you now than it did a few pages ago? Remember, this book is just a beginning for you. In this section, I've put a rough edge on the ax of your writing; now you must hone it to a fine edge by practicing the nuances of our language.

Speaking of the nuances of the language, sentence length, hard consonant and vowel sounds, and meter aren't the only tools in the writer's toolbox when it comes to controlling how quickly the reader gets through the work. Because every mark of punctuation creates a pause of some length, the writer can speed up the reader (and his heart rate, conveying a stronger sense of emotion) by combining the right words and sentences with the right punctuation.

The Importance of Punctuation in Dialogue

After the ability to use lines, circles, and arcs to form letters, and the ability to form words from those letters, punctuation is the most important tool in the writer's toolbox. Because of the subliminal and peripheral messages punctuation conveys to the reader, you can even use it to reveal the characters' mood and intent.

The main purpose of dialogue is to convey the emotions of the characters and to manipulate the emotions of the reader. To that end, after we finish the discussion of how to manipulate reader speed through the use of punctuation (or the lack of it), we'll discuss various methods for using punctuation to convey emotion more directly and less subliminally.

Note: Some would argue the main purpose of dialogue is to advance the story line, but I'll stick by my guns regarding conveying and manipulating emotion. If the story is **plot** driven, emotion (as delivered through dialogue) will cause the reader to remain loyal, struggling through each conflict with the characters all the way to the resolution; if the story is character driven, well, the dialogue had *better* evoke emotion in the reader, hadn't it? Characters advance the story line partly through dialogue and partly through personality, and the narrator advances it partly through descriptive narrative and partly through suggestion and innuendo.

A Brief Refresher

Punctuation consists of four categories of marks. Each of the first three categories creates a pause:

> The period, question mark, exclamation point and colon create a long pause.
> The semicolon, em dash, and parentheses create a medium pause.
> The comma creates a short pause.

Long-pause punctuation commonly is used only after a complete thought; **medium-pause punctuation** is used where a long pause is not necessary and a short pause is not enough, most often to indicate a linkage between two sections of a passage. **Short-pause punctuation**, the comma, typically is used to coordinate components of a sentence.

The fourth category is **spelling punctuation** (apostrophe, hyphen). It affects the spelling of words and does not create a pause at all. In fact, the reader will actually read through two words combined into one hyphenated word more quickly than through the same two words without a hyphen. As you will see shortly, punctuation (or the lack of it) can be used in nontraditional ways to achieve some amazing effects. Just remember, you should always consider the effect your punctuation will have on the reader.

For example, the semicolon is used to join two or more closely related complete thoughts. Take a look at this excerpt from *Punctuation for Writers*:

> Mary found out she was pregnant last week. John left
> for college yesterday.

> Mary found out she was pregnant last week; John left
> for college yesterday.

> In the first example, although we might think the second sentence is related to the first, we can't be sure without reading more to glean information from the overall context. But in the second example, we are absolutely certain John left as a direct result of Mary's discovery of her pregnancy. The semicolon in the second example, by connecting the two sentences with a medium pause, indicates that cause-and-effect relationship.

Now let's continue our discussion of how to manipulate reader speed, this time from a standpoint of punctuation.

Using Punctuation to Affect Reader Speed

The writer who recognizes punctuation as a nuance of the language has another invaluable tool with which to manipulate the reading of her work; through her use of punctuation, she can convey the emotions of her characters and cause the emotions of the reader to wax or wane. And if great writing is about anything at all, it's about conveying and controlling emotion.

Remember that the reader's response to punctuation is involuntarily. Think back to the last time you read a newspaper story. Did you notice the commas that were not supposed to be there? Of course you did. You had to stop, go back and re-read the sentence a second time after omitting the offending comma. The point is, the reader cannot read *through* a comma or other mark of punctuation; he *must* pause for a certain length of time before he can resume reading.

Although it's most often important to get your punctuation right, sometimes it's just as important to get it not right, but to do so intentionally. That is, sometimes it's better to break the punctuation rules to create a certain effect in the reader.

Below, I offer two very different examples, one from a friend's short story, "After a Time," and one from my own, "Soft as a Breeze." My friend uses the colon, a piece of long-pause punctuation, in a very unconventional way to force the reader's attention onto certain details, thereby also heightening the reader's experience. He also speeds the reader along by using very few other marks of punctuation. In my own I make use of a lack of punctuation (combined with harsh words and sounds) to speed the reader through the work so he can experience the heightened emotions of the character in the story rather than simply being a passive observer.

First, an excerpt from Jason Gurley's short story, "After a Time," from his first collection, *Close Program* (Pixel Press, 2001). In this scene, the narrator has just called an old friend he's recognized by his name, Robert, only to discover that the man has changed his name. Notice that Mr. Gurley's unique placement of the colon not only adds to the intrigue and suspense of the story, but that it also adds a somehow necessary emphasis to the phrase that follows it. Finally, notice that Mr. Gurley's use of commas to run sentences together causes us to speed through the passages that aren't interrupted by his unorthodox use of the colon:

"It's Garrett now," he said darkly, and let the big door grind shut, then leaned on it and stared up at the same sky I had been admiring, and I wondered if the rust on the door was staining his bald head. "Garrett Holman."

"I'm confused," I said, and I was, but I thought that I knew why Robert Mitchell had become Garrett Holman, and my thinking led me back to: sweaty, leafy jungles full of scared white boys in grease-paint and torn camos, back to: sludgy swamps that killed more men than Charlie did, seeping into boots and socks and infecting unsuspecting feet, back to: napalm rain-showers and near-insane sergeants, and I knew why Robert became Garrett: to escape.

But there was no escaping the skin graft that patched together his cheek and his lip, on both sides of his face like a flesh-tone manhole cover that's been warped and adjusted by the traffic and weather, only the adjusting here had been done by a bad surgeon.

"I gotta go back in," Robert said, and the door wouldn't open from the outside, and he knocked lightly, but: nobody answered, and he knocked harder, but: there was nobody there, and he pounded, but: nobody came to his rescue, and he was stuck in the cool night with a memory he didn't want to talk to.

"Robert," I said quietly, and when he turned, his face seemed whiter beneath the caked-on makeup, makeup that couldn't hide the strange, shifting layer of skin on either side of his face, like a mud pie slapped on by a child, and he breathed deeply, over and over, and I said his name again.

"I don't want to talk to you," he answered, "I don't, I don't — "

"My name is Greg," I said, and he closed his eyes and paranoid leaks sliced through his makeup and trickled in smeary white rivulets down his neck and stained his crisp white collar. "My name is Greg," I said, "and we were together in the war, and we were friends, and we promised each other we'd always be friends — and now you can't talk to me?"

Robert slid down the door to the damp concrete, and splayed there with his greasy face in his shaking hands and said, "No, no, go away, go away," and after a time, I: touched his shoulder and said, "Ro — " and he shoved me away, violently, and I banged off of the alley wall, and my back hurt, the metal plate hurt, and Robert — Garrett — began to scream like a little girl, and after a time, I: hung my head and walked away, and after a time, I: thought I had forgotten about Robert, but: nobody forgets about those they slept in the jungle with; it just doesn't happen.

As you can see, Mr. Gurley used the colon intentionally to achieve a particular effect in the reader. Notice that the odd usage does not detract from the story and, in fact, greatly enhances its emotional impact.

The next example is an excerpt from "Soft as a Breeze," in which I tried to let the reader experience a few hellish seconds, at least emotionally, along with the character. Because the emotion in this story builds from almost nothing to a fever pitch, then drops sharply off, I included the introductory dialogue to set the scene and the last paragraph to ease the reader out of the scene. To avoid confusion, I'll tell you now that *Digger* is Jimmy's nickname:

Digger brought me a beer that night, soft again. Wantin' to help a little bit, I think. Thought maybe my nerves were shot or somethin'.

"Stan?" he said out of the dark, whispery like. I looked up easy, not jumpy, 'cause it was more like a breeze. Not like a snap or a body movin' past a blade of elephant grass or nothin', but like a real breeze. Just soft. Like it's almost there but not really.

"Yeah?" I couldn't do it as soft as he could.

The breeze passed me a beer, then smiled and settled next to me on his heels. "You okay?" Whispery.

"Yeah, No problem." A raindrop filtered off a leaf and streaked across my glasses.

Quiet. "Everything works out, huh? I been here eleven months and ain't never come that close."

"Everything works out," I said. Still couldn't get as soft as he could.

Soft. "Well, I gotta get back home." Lifting himself from the ground, the breeze drifted toward its sleeping bag.

"See you in the mornin', Digger."

"See you."

Being there was mostly boring. Long periods of nothin' to do but wait for somethin' to happen. It was quiet and soft and sweet, a lot like Jimmy, 'til that one scalding, blinding-white instant when all hell breaks loose and then is reconfined. All in that split second. I mean there's a big lead-up that's sort of excitin' and scary and lasts longer than time when things are happening all around you and you're diving for a hole and grabbing your rifle and trying to stick a magazine in upside down and throwing ammo to your buddy and dodging sounds all at once, kind of like a spooked house cat. But it's still okay 'cause it ain't happening directly *to* you.

Then there's that scalding-hot second of pure hell when the whole damn mess centers on you, just you, when you're all by yourself and so is your buddy who's only a foot away, when you think the earth is spitting little puffs of dirt at you 'til an eternity-long split second later when you remember it's bullets, when all the rain in every drizzly, miserable cloud on earth is falling within a two-foot radius of the center of your head and everything and everyone is screaming at you or past you and you can't do anything as fast or as good as you have every day of your life like duck or run or get out of the mud or find a trigger or remember a friend who pulled you out of a tunnel two weeks ago, then — then the instant ends and you're alive. And you've got to get capable again.

You start to stop shaking and you think of a cigarette and reach for one, then Mom flashes a disapproving look through your mind but you reach anyway, then you want to joke with your friend, show him you're both still bad, tell him Charlie'd rather sandpaper a bear's ass in a phone booth than mess with you and he smiles kind of soft in your mind and you want to offer to split that extra beer in your pack with him, you know? *Split a beer with the wind* you think maybe help *his* nerves a little bit and you smile, so you think to reach for it but decide to joke first and get the beer in a second and you're smiling and turning your head and opening your mouth to tell him about bear's asses in phone booths —

But his face is gone.

Then your body is turning inside out and you can't hear and all you feel is screaming and scalding water on your cheeks even in the rain that's too damn hard and cold and miserable to care about anything and four guys jump on you like the rain and the wind, hard like thugs, take your breath like a gale like a damn firestorm, not soft not like a breeze and they yell things like *Shhh!* and *Shut up!* and they use your name like they know you but you scream right through their hands right through the blood and bones grimy meat of their filthy, muddy, bony, f**king hands. Screaming.

Screaming for a breeze, just a soft little breeze. But the breeze is gone.

The louie came up the next day with his head down. Said how Digger took a round to the side of his head, how it looked like it hit his right cheekbone. And he said how he was real sorry, not because he *had* to, like some lieutenants, but because he really was sorry. But he had nothin' to be sorry for. Hell, I mean, even Jimmy wasn't soft enough there, you know? Nobody is.

Did the lack of punctuation cause you to speed through the passage? Did you get a sense of the character's emotional state? Did you perhaps *share* the character's emotional state? Did you sense the almost stark drama of the short last sentence?

Other than the fact that both stories are based on the horrors of warfare (strictly a coincidence), do you see any other similarities? Are there similarities in structure? In use of punctuation? In tone? What emotions, if any, did you experience while reading the excerpts? Did you share the emotions of the characters? Were your emotions the same from one story to the next? Similar? Vastly different? These are things you need to consider when striving to make an impact on your reader.

Conveying Emotion Directly Through Punctuation

Until now, we've discussed the more subliminal ways to convey the characters' emotions to the reader through sentence length, the unorthodox use of punctuation, and a lack of punctuation. Now we're going to see how we can use particular sentence structures and particular pieces of punctuation to convey that emotion more directly.

Earlier, I touched on the em dash and the ellipsis, but I didn't mention that either of them can be used to inject strong emotion into dialogue. The em dash, which is formed by typing two hyphens -- like this -- or, in MS Word, by pressing Ctrl and Alt and the hyphen key on the number pad, is used to indicate an interruption, either of one character by another or of a character by himself (a break in thought). The ellipsis, which consists of three periods with a space before and after each, is used in the middle of a sentence of dialogue to indicate halting speech, as if a character were unsure of himself or striving to say precisely the right thing or at the end of a sentence of dialogue to indicate a voice trailing off.

Here's a brief example of one character interrupting another as indicated by an em dash:

> "John, I just don't understand why you think this is such a big deal. It isn't like we don't have the money. For goodness' sake, it's been —"
> "All right, all right! Get the tickets and we'll go to Hawaii. Just let me finish what I'm doing here, okay?"

As you can see, because it provides only a brief pause instead of the long pause created by a period, for example, the em dash indicates the suddenness with which an interruption occurs. The same effect occurs when a character interrupts himself, either to begin talking with a different character, as in the first example

> "So after the first couple beers, we were getting pretty loose. Well, I waltzed up to the boss and told him I wouldn't even consider a transfer to — Hey, John! What's going on? How's your head?"
> "Not bad. Quite a night. You doing all right?"
> "About the same. You know Henry, don't you? I was just telling him we should all get together for some golf this Saturday."

or because he suddenly has another thought, as in this example. Also notice the halting speech indicated by the ellipsis in this example:

> "I was thinking about our honeymoon. How would you feel about Niagara Falls? You know, it's supposed to be — No, wait! How about Hawaii? I mean, we can afford it . . . unless you'd rather go to Niagara."

Finally, when you use an ellipsis at the end of a sentence of dialogue to indicate a voice trailing off, follow it with the appropriate end punctuation, usually a period or question mark. This example shows the ellipsis used in both ways:

> "I know you wanted to visit Hawaii this summer, Megan, and I hate to disappoint you, but . . . well, the money . . . ."

Remember, the period following the second ellipsis is just a period — the appropriate end punctuation — that occurs after, and separate of, the ellipsis.

Now let's look at some specific, in-depth techniques.

The Barrage

We've already seen that longer sentences convey more or stronger emotion. A longer sequence of sentences delivered by one character will do the same thing. The level of emotion, of course, is in part dependent on the subject of the **barrage**. Take a look at the snippets of dialogue below. Remember, our aim is to convey the emotion of the character(s) and affect the emotions of the reader:

> "What do you mean you don't know whether we ought to move? Don't you realize what this promotion means for me, for us? I mean, is moving to Seattle really so inconvenient that you're willing to give up a raise this large? And for what, just so you can stay in this lousy desert? Well?"

Notice that I intentionally omitted any descriptive narrative passages. With no narrative hints, what can you tell about the emotional state of Character A, the character who's speaking? What about the emotional state of the implied (nonspeaking) Character B? What are the genders of the characters?

Here's my intent: I repeated the same sentence structure five times in quick succession, allowing no interruptions from the other character or the narrator, not even so much as a tag line. In that succession, four long questions are followed by a very short one. (We've seen this technique before, yes?) I intended to convey (1) Character A's furious or indignant or incredulous disbelief, (2) Character B's fearful or sinister or melancholy silence, and (3) a highly stressful situation that both characters probably (mistakenly) thought had been resolved sometime before this conversation. Whether Character A is furious, indignant, or incredulous and Character B is fearful, sinister, or melancholy depends on the rest of the story line. If you want to indicate a little more firmly that Character B is being verbally brow-beaten, you can do so by using some other techniques that convey emotion, albeit techniques still driven primarily by punctuation.

Interrupting the Barrage

Using the em dash to indicate one character interrupting another builds tension quickly and makes the reader lean in. Let's continue with the same example, still using the lengthy sentences to convey emotion, but this time with interruptions. Notice that interruption also is a good way to indicate a struggle for control:

> "What do you mean you don't know whether we ought to move? Don't you realize what this promotion means for me, for us?"
> "But —"
> "I mean, is moving to Seattle really so inconvenient that you're willing to give up a raise this large?"
> "It's just that —"
> "And for what, just so you can stay in this lousy desert? Well?"

The interruption is an effective way to build tension and engage the reader because it's abrupt, and it's abrupt because we use the em dash. When you compare this example with the one under "Barrage," do you feel the tension of the interruption? Allowing the Character B to interrupt Character A twice and letting the reader see Character A ignore those interruptions conveys more strongly the intensity of Character A's emotions and establishes him as being in control of the conversation. Of course, we don't know at this point whether Character A is being rude or whether he's just so wrapped up in the emotion of the moment that he doesn't even hear the interruptions. But we can punch it up a bit:

> "What do you mean you don't know whether we ought to move? Don't you realize what this promotion means for me, for us?"
> "But —"
> "I mean, is moving to Seattle really so inconvenient that you're willing to give up a raise this large?"
> "It's just that —"
> "It's just what? Just so you can stay in this lousy desert? Well?"

Because Character A used part of Character B's dialogue against her, now we're certain he has heard at least the second interruption and has chosen to use it as a springboard to berate Character B. Now let's carry it a step further:

> "What do you mean you don't know whether we ought to move? Don't you realize what this promotion means for me, for us?"
>
> "But —"
>
> "I mean, is moving to Seattle really so inconvenient that you're willing to give up a raise this large?"
>
> "It's just that —"
>
> "It's just what? Just so you can stay in this lousy desert? Well?"
>
> "I just can't talk —"
>
> "Yeah, yeah, sure! Now let's go on for awhile about how you can't talk to me when I'm in this condition! What condition? Wanting to make things better for my family?"
>
> "John, I —"
>
> "I just don't understand what's so bad about trying to make the best living I can for my family. What's so wrong with —"
>
> "John, I want a divorce."

Blam! Right in the gut! In this lengthy passage of dialogue, the reader is reeled in, closer and closer, paying more and more attention (weren't you?), trying to see what's going to happen between this bickering couple, and then we hit him with a short, terse line. Did the final sentence evoke a sense of drama? Once again our ghost returns: *A longer sentence conveys emotion; a shorter sentence evokes a sense of drama.* As you can see, that's especially true if the short sentence occurs after several longer, emotion-building sentences.

Wandering Off-Topic

In the previous example, we also see Character A attempting to further bully (barrage) Character B by *wandering off-topic* for a moment, basically filibustering, in the paragraph that begins "Yeah, yeah, sure!"

That paragraph has nothing to do with the current argument, which is about whether the couple will relocate. Notice too that just before the dramatic punch at the end, Character B reverses the trend of the dialogue, interrupting Character A. This sudden switch is another subliminal dramatic punch for the reader. Before this, Character B has been mostly subdued, but not only did Character B win the conversation, she also assumed control of the overall situation.

You'll also notice we pulled off this trick without the use of so much as a tag line, much less any longer descriptive narrative. As I mention in Chapter 1, use tag lines — the little *he said, she said* narrative bits — only when they're absolutely necessary to let the reader know which character is speaking. In the passage above, did you ever get confused about which character is speaking? If not, we didn't need tag lines.

To deepen or strengthen the emotion of this scene, let's give the characters names and use just a bit of descriptive narrative:

> John clenched his right hand into a fist around the stems of the roses he'd brought Mary. "What do you mean you don't know whether we ought to move? Don't you realize what this promotion means for me, for us?"
>
> "But —"
>
> "I mean, is moving to Seattle really so inconvenient that you're willing to give up a raise this large?"
>
> "It's just that —"
>
> "It's just what? Just so you can stay in this lousy desert?" The roses hit the far wall. "Well?"
>
> "I just can't talk —"
>
> "Yeah, yeah, sure! Now let's go on for awhile about how you can't talk to me when I'm in this condition! What condition? Wanting to make things better for my family?"
>
> "John, I —"
>
> "I just don't understand what's so bad about trying to make the best living I can for my family. What's so wrong with —"

"John, I want a divorce."

"What? You want . . . a divorce? Mary, what —"

Mary picked up her purse. "I'll be at the Marriott. Don't wait up." The door closed on a silent house.

All right, so I added a bit more dialogue too. Did you get a better picture of what's going on from the brief descriptive narrative passages? Did you get a better picture of John's emotional state? Did you get a sense of finality when Mary picked up her purse? When did the momentum change hands? You'll notice that once Mary interrupted John the first time and shocked him into a stammering, momentary silence — his halting speech is indicated by the ellipsis — she interrupted him again and then told him how it was going to be. We didn't have to say *Mary took control of the conversation.* (That would be telling, not showing.) Instead, we implied the change of power by letting the reader see who interrupted whom. For more information on the proper use of descriptive narrative, see Chapter 1.

Volleying

Some of the strongest, most emotion-filled dialogue is the result of **volleying**, two or more characters going at each other without interruption or with only occasional interruption. The volleying dialogue can consist of characters berating each other, arguing (as in the following example), or firing questions back and forth. Remember these main characteristics of the verbal volley: The amount and strength of dialogue from each character should be roughly equivalent, and you should use as few narrative bits as possible so the reader is allowed to speed through the dialogue along with the characters, thereby heightening the emotional effect. Generally, the longer the characters exchange shots without one gaining the upper hand, the stronger and more effective the technique. To illustrate volleying, I've used a variation of the previous example:

"What do you mean you don't know whether we ought to move? Don't you realize what this promotion means for me, for us?"

"I meant exactly what I said. I'm not sure."

"Is moving to Seattle really so inconvenient that you're willing to give up a raise this large?"

"Is the money all you think about? This is my home, John!"

"So you refuse to move just so you can stay in this lousy desert? Well?"

"I just can't talk to you . . . ."

"Yeah, yeah, sure! Now let's go on for awhile about how you can't talk to me when I'm in this condition! What condition? Wanting to make things better for my family?"

"Don't change the subject. Besides, I didn't say anything about your stupid condition. I said I can't talk to you!"

"I just don't understand what's so bad about trying to make the best living I can for my family. What's so wrong with —"

"You just don't listen. You just never —"

"What? What do you mean I never —"

"John, I want a divorce."

"What? Mary, we can —"

"No, John. I'll be at the Marriott. Don't wait up."

Do you see the changing dynamic of the dialogue? Does the level of intensity change a bit now that the exchange is more evenly split between the characters?

Volleying also is an excellent way to inject anger, humor, sarcasm, smugness or any of several other emotions into a story line. In the first example, a husband has just come home from work:

"Honey, I brought a couple friends home for supper. What're we having?"

"I don't know. What are you planning to fix?"

In this one, Dad has just come home from work and planted a kiss on his teenage daughter's forehead:

"Hi Sweety. How was your day?"
"Well, I got a date for the dance on Friday."
"Great! Who is it?"
"Remember that guy who fixed our fence last summer?"
"Isn't he a little old for you?"
"He's barely thirty, Dad."

All of the above snippets of dialogue were rendered emotion filled by use of words and sentences that flew by very quickly; the repetition of a particular sentence structure; long, austerely punctuated sentences; the use of certain subordinate words to indicate the initial subjugation of Character B (*But, It's just*); the use of interruption (indicated by the em dash) to show the strength and weakness of the characters; the use of halting speech (indicated by the ellipsis) to show a sudden, uncharacteristic lack of confidence; and the use of short, firm, terse statements to indicate that the weaker character had become the stronger.

Creative Nonfiction and Dialogue

Just so you know, these techniques needn't be limited to fiction or to angry tension. You can also use them in nonfiction and/or to create humorous tension. Since you've already seen the techniques, I won't explain them again, but for a final example for this chapter, let me offer you some light reading — an essay that falls into the category of exaggeration to say the least. "The Importance of Writing Naked" first appeared as a humor column in the now-defunct *Candlelight Poetry Journal*. (Imagine for a moment — a humor column in a poetry journal.) I include it here not only as an example, but because it contains invaluable advice for writers. Enjoy.

The Importance of Writing Naked
(and the unusual Drawbacks thereof)

Despite what you may think, I was actually writing both prose and poetry long before I started writing this column.

And like most writers and poets, I gleaned a wealth of valuable information from other, more advanced, writers over the years. Golden rules like "Write what you know" and "Write in different positions" and "Pace while you're writing" and "Clean the candy smear off your manuscript before you send it in" and "Never write in first person" and later "Always write in first person" and "Never turn your back in the shower when your buddy has a damp towel twisted up in his hands." Okay, maybe that last one doesn't fit, but it's good advice and I'm sure you get the gist.

The overall idea is that heeding the advice of more experienced writers will usually save you some time and keep you out of trouble. But one of the most often repeated tidbits of wisdom I have heard is that writers who wish to be even vaguely successful should strive to write naked. *Write naked?* Yeah, that one threw me, too. Apparently, though, it didn't throw me far enough to avoid the problems it would cause.

Most writers take advice pretty well, but we seldom take it immediately. Instead, we mull it over awhile. It sits on a back burner in our mind until it ripens. Sometimes it sits back there until it starts to rot, but writers prefer *ferment.* How many times have you heard writers and poets talk about letting an idea ferment? Then, one day when the writer's mood, the piece he's working on, and the fermenting advice gel BAM! the advice kicks in. And what can you do? The timing is right, the moon's lined up with the third planet of the fourth star system on the right in the Villanellian galaxy, your muse has turned her impish back, and your editor's yelling about deadlines. So like any good writer, you Go For It. All well and good, provided that you first ascertain *advisory intent*; that is, make sure the advice meant specifically what you took it to mean. There's no substitute for measuring twice before you cut once. (I'm not sure what that means, but it sounds good.)

So anyway, I was stuck, and thought there must be a way to unclog my mind. I began running down all the advice I'd heard. I'd already tried writing the poem in first person, then *not* in first person. I'd tried pacing while writing, and writing while lying on my back with my feet on my chair and my journal propped up on my knees. I'd already tried writing what I knew, and even what I suspected. Nothing worked. Blocked I was, and blocked I would remain. Then, like a banshee screaming out from the cobwebs of my mind, came the one piece of advice I hadn't tried: *write naked*. After all, it's rumored that Papa Hemingway wrote while standing in his underwear at a drawing table, right? And according to Robert Hendrickson in *The Literary Life and Other Curiosities* (Harcourt, 1994), William Blake, Samuel Boyse, D.H. Lawrence, Victor Hugo, Ben Franklin, James Whitcomb Riley, Robin Moore, and John Cheever also wrote in the nude or semi-nude for various reasons at one time or another. So I'm thinking *What's the big deal? Not only will I write naked, but I'll be in excellent company!* I disrobed, right there in front of my computer, gaily flinging my shirt hither and my trousers yon (when writers fling stuff, they fling it hither and yon) and kicking my shoes and socks to a temporary resting place against the far wall. So far, so good. That's when my wife came in. She's my immediate tie to the wide world of sanity, a world from which my departure seems continually imminent.

Anyway, she comes waltzing into the room with a smile on her face and a thought to share. "Honey," she said. "You should come see this guy on television. You'll never believe what he's — Harvey, *What* are you *doing*?"

I absolutely beamed. "I'm getting ready to write naked."

She took in the discarded clothing in a glance. "Naked?"

"Naked."

Her hands moved to her hips. "And is there some particular reason?"

"Well, I was stuck. I was writing this poem and I got stuck. You know. Blocked. Then I remembered somebody once told me if I got stuck, I should —"

"You should write naked?"

"Well . . . yes."

She handed me my trousers. "Put these on."

"But if I put those on, I won't be able to —"

"Put them on!"

"But I —"

"*Now!*"

I'm thinking, *Pick your battles, Harv. She'll go back into the living room in a few minutes. Then you can get naked and write your heart out.*

The simple act of pulling my trousers up over my hips and fastening the button had a soothing effect on her. "Sweety," she said quietly, stroking my forehead. "You misunderstood. To write naked means to bare your *soul.*"

"I know, but you just said —"

"No, Sweety. You're still not quite getting it." Patience is her virtue. "To write naked, you bare your *soul,* not your body."

"Not my body?"

"No."

"So I don't have to get undressed?"

"No."

New information. "Hmmm. Guess I looked pretty silly, huh?"

"Not half as silly as the time you tried to walk from here to the park on your hands so you'd know how Atlas felt."

"That was pretty dumb, wasn't it?"

"Good thing that car missed you. Or the time you pretended to sleepwalk so you'd know what it was like before you wrote an essay about it."

"Yeah, that was a little off too."

"Or that time you —"

"Okay, okay! I get the point already!"

"Are you sure?"

"Sure of what?"

"Sure you got the point?"

"Yeah." I all but purred.

"Okay. I'm going back to the living room now. Let's not have a replay of this, okay?"

"Okay. So what's the guy on TV doing anyway?"

"What guy?"

"The one you came in to tell me about."

"I forget. Besides, that was fiction. You're real and you've got him beat by a long shot. I guess it's true what they say about fact being stranger than fiction, isn't it?"

"I guess."

She bent to kiss me on the forehead. "Remember, Sir: Bare the *soul* — leave the body in disguise."

Summary

We've seen that the purpose of dialogue, and of all writing, is to capture the reader for a period of time. We've seen that no matter which traits or methods or formulae we study or practice, to write successfully, everything we put on the page must be placed with a thought for how it will affect the reader. All other considerations are secondary.

To that end, we've learned to convey the emotions of our characters and evoke emotion in our readers. We've been made aware of the nuances of our language, from the sounds of individual letters and words as they're pronounced in the reader's mind to the nano-pause created by a comma. We know we can effectively speed up the human heart by displaying a series of lightly punctuated, long sentences. And we know we can slam the reader into a dramatic wall by planting a short, terse statement at the end.

These are the nuances of the language. The good news is that once you've consciously used them for awhile, their use will become second nature to you. As Penny Porter wrote, now "it's just a matter of keeping a promise, living up to your dialogue."

Chapter 3   Narrative

Narrative is non-dialogue text that advances the story line while maintaining or heightening reader interest. The main factors of reader interest are curiosity and tension. The interested reader wants to see what's just around the corner, and he wants it to be something other than what he expects.

Narrative Versus Dialogue

It is the writer's job to keep the reader reading or, more specifically, it is the writer's job not to interrupt the reader. Now, imagine that you have written the most engaging novel since some ancient guy first noticed he could make an *A* with two long sticks and a shorter one. Imagine that it is all but impossible for the reader to close your book without immediately longing to open it again. Even so, every time the reader is pulled from the story by the door bell, the telephone, a barking dog, the narrator, or some other maddening intrusions, you run the risk she will put down your book and not pick it up again.

Just as door bells, telephones, and barking dogs are intrusive, so is narrative, *always*, to some degree. Remember that. There are more than enough intrusions out there to distract your reader from your work. Obviously, the less intrusive the narrator is, the better. After all, why interrupt a person who's concentrating breathlessly on your work?

In almost every situation, some narrative is necessary, of course. After all, that exciting opening scene is often written in narrative. So my intent isn't to try to convince you that narrative is bad and should never be used. On the contrary, when it isn't overused or used poorly, narrative is an effective tool. Just keep a few things in mind:

1. The narrator (either the author or a character) always speaks

directly to the reader (a distraction) and usually does so from outside the story line — *your* story line.

a. If the narrator is not a character, every time he speaks to the reader it's as if he walked into the room and tapped the reader on the shoulder. The worst case of this is when the non-character narrator tells the reader what one of the characters could as easily (and more naturally) have told the other (and the reader by extension). This problem is discussed in detail in Chapter 4.

b. Even when the narrator is a character, he still is speaking directly to the reader. Consequentially, *everything the narrator says must be germane to the story.* I can't repeat often enough that every word, phrase, sentence, paragraph, and bit of punctuation the writer puts on the page should be placed carefully and with a thought for how it will affect the reader and/or how the reader will react. Writers must take special care to avoid providing too much information. We've all heard the long-standing advice to *Write what you know,* but that doesn't mean you should write *everything* you know, especially in one story or novel. It just won't fit. We'll discuss this problem in Chapter 4.

c. In what the narrator relates, he also must balance (1) giving the reader enough information to keep from confusing him with (2) giving the reader too much information, which makes the reader feel the author (not the narrator) believes himself superior. This is what editors mean when they advise a writer not to "beat the reader over the head" with information. For an in-depth discussion and examples, see Chapter 4.

2. Narrative is a one-sided conversation. When the reader eavesdrops on a conversation between characters, he doesn't expect to receive all the answers; after all, he's eavesdropping. If he listens long enough, he'll find out what he needs to know. Suspense builds, and the reader is hooked. But when the author relates information directly to the reader that would be better related through character dialogue, it's strictly a one-sided conversation from which the reader derives little satisfaction.

When receiving narrative, the reader is not an active participant in the story. He is neither an eavesdropper of a conversation between characters nor a sleuth who is using his own mind to determine what's going on; when he is receiving narrative, the reader is a passive listener. The difference between being an active reader or a passive listener is like the difference between watching a Shakespearean play on stage or listening while someone simply reads it aloud.

Narrative as an Adjunct to Dialogue

Great fiction requires the suspension of disbelief. Dialogue is among the best tools for suspending a reader's disbelief because, in the written word, it equates with action and enlists the reader as an eavesdropper. However, it's difficult to make a reader believe the dialogue is real when the characters are static, as actors on a stage, standing face to face and simply reading their lines aloud from a script. In other words, even the most dialogue-driven story lines require the occasional (and intentional) use of narrative to provide color and movement, at least in the form of tag lines and brief introductory and interruptive descriptive narratives (see Chapter 1).

In some stories, much more narrative is necessary. If you want to relate a story directly to the reader, for example, virtually making the reader a non-speaking character who is the audience for a monologue, narrative is the perfect tool (see "Using Narrative Instead of Dialogue," below). Because dialogue engages the reader in every instance, I advise you always to determine whether narrative is necessary. That is, *when you use narrative, as when you use dialogue or an exclamation point or an ellipsis or italics, use it with a specific intent.*

There is a vast difference between necessary narrative and unnecessary narrative. But given that you do need to write narrative for whatever reason, make it as action-packed as possible. That is, use the active voice rather than the passive voice. Just as dialogue works well because it equates with action, so should your narrative convey action through crispness, brevity, and the use of nouns, action verbs, and effective descriptive adjectives and adverbs.

By *brevity* I mean you should narrate only as necessary to inform the reader, then stop. But what about those nouns, action verbs, and descriptive adjectives and adverbs? As I wrote in Chapter 6 of the first book in the Thorough Primer series, *Punctuation for Writers,*

> Whenever you write a noun, you place a picture in the reader's mind. When you follow the noun with an *action verb,* the picture moves and actually shows the reader what's going on. This is why you often hear fiction instructors say you should show, not tell, the reader what's going on. They probably should say *Let the reader see what's going on; don't tell him what's going on.* When you don't have to tell a reader what's going on in the story, when he can see it for himself through your use of action verbs, you'll also need and use fewer descriptive adjectives and adverbs.

Using Action Verbs to Create a Mental Movie

So when you write a noun, you put a picture in the reader's mind, but it's a static picture. It doesn't move. Try it yourself. Read these nouns and see whether they move in your mind:

cat	horse	train
sedan	ship	printer

Now let's add an action verb or two and see what happens. The nouns I'm using as subjects are in bold and the verbs are in italics:

the **cat** *overbalanced* and *fell* from the sill / *nestled* on a sunny rug

the **horse** *paced* around the track / *galloped* over the hill the **train** *labored* up the steep slope / *fled* from the tunnel

the **sedan** *shrieked* to a halt / *purred* at a red light

the **ship** *tore* from its moorings / *creaked* against the coral reef

the **printer** *whirred* and *hummed* / *stippled* holes into the top layer

I provided at least two action verbs for each subject so you could see the picture change from one situation to the next. Your reader won't know all of this is going on; she'll just not want to put down your book.

One of my favorite examples is this: How would you like to read a book full of sentences like the following?

John was angry.

Do you get any sense of John or what's going on in the scene from that sentence? How about this?

John was very very very angry.

Does the addition of the repeated *very* help? Do you know any more now about the scene than you knew a moment ago? No. And take my word for it, replacing the period with an exclamation point won't work either. Because we used the state-of-being verb *was* in the sentence, then attempted to strengthen it by adding *very*, these sentences *tell* the reader about John rather than letting the reader *see* the scene for himself through the use of action verbs. (More on state-of-being verbs later in the chapter.) How about this:

John kicked in the door, stormed up the stairs, slapped Maria, and hurled Joaquin through a window.

Now do you see what's going on in the scene? That's the difference action verbs can make in your writing. Notice, too, that not one time did the word *angry* or *mad* or even *upset* appear, but do you doubt John's state of mind? You might also have noticed that there are no adjectives or adverbs in the sentence. In addition to bringing life to your narrative by providing action, good action verbs also can help set the tone or mood of a scene.

Using Action Verbs to Set the Tone

Only action verbs can create the tone of a scene, whether foreboding or fear, warmth or comfort, joy or despair. Even without an accompanying noun to begin and therefore complete the picture, verbs like *sang*, *danced*, and *leapt* lend a sense of joy to a scene. Verbs like *crept*, *slouched*, and *fell* provide a sense of fear or foreboding, and *nestled*, *rocked*, and *eased* tend to lend a sense of warmth or comfort. Consider the effect of these verbs also in context of the letters and sounds of which they're composed (see "The Sounds of Letters and Words" in Chapter 2).

You'll notice that these verbs act on the reader's emotions to some degree despite their context. For example, even in an otherwise happy or joyful setting, *crept* gives the reader a tinge of foreboding:

> Thinking the batter might attempt a sacrifice bunt, the third baseman crept toward home plate.

See? Even though we're talking about a baseball game, *crept* scares us a little. In this instance, we might consider using a verb like *slipped* or *inched* or even *moved* instead, unless we *want* the reader to pick up that little sense of foreboding.

Obviously, these are only a few of the action verbs that you can use to directly and subliminally affect the reader's emotional state. Discovery is among the chief joys of the writer, so I'll leave you to find others.

Using Descriptive Adjectives and Adverbs

We've discussed nouns and action verbs, but what about those descriptive adjectives and adverbs? I mentioned earlier that when you use action verbs, you'll need and use fewer descriptive adjectives and adverbs. Actually, the unnecessary ones will fall away naturally, leaving only those that are necessary to further describe the scene. Let's take a look at how you can effectively use adjectives and adverbs in the structure of the sentence.

First, let's consider what we mean by the *necessary use* of descriptive adjectives and adverbs in the context of using action verbs. In your story, a sentence reads, "The clumsy cat overbalanced and fell from the window sill." Because of the action verb *overbalanced*, you don't need the adjective *clumsy*, do you? But if the cat isn't simply clumsy and why he fell from the window sill is important to the story line, *wounded* might be a necessary adjective. Also, chances are that the particular type of cat isn't important to the scene, but if it does make a difference, use descriptive adjectives: "The chartreuse cat overbalanced and fell from the window sill."

Let's look briefly at descriptive adverbs. These almost always end in *ly*, and often you can form an adverb by adding *ly* to an adjective. Adjectives, by and large, modify (color) nouns, pronouns, and other adjectives; adverbs modify verbs, adjectives, and other adverbs. (Descriptive adverbs are most commonly used to modify verbs.) For example, the first sentence of this paragraph could have begun, "Let's take a brief look . . ." with *brief*, an adjective, modifying *look*, in this case a noun. The verb is *take*. In "Let's look briefly at . . . ," the verb is *look* and it's modified by *briefly*, an adverb formed by adding *ly* to an adjective. Adverbs are handy for coloring the action just a little. For example, "He rode into the sunset" is a perfectly fine sentence. But "He rode slowly into the sunset" and "He rode quickly into the sunset" provide the reader with vastly different pictures. The main thing to remember about adverbs, like adjectives, is that if they aren't important to the scene or story, don't include them. Happily, if they aren't important to the scene, they often won't include themselves.

The flip side of that, of course, is that if they are necessary, use them. That's why they exist. You'll remember that in the example of John we used in "Using Action Verbs to Create a Mental Movie," there were no adjectives or adverbs. They weren't necessary, so we omitted them. But what if we wanted the reader to get a little better idea of John's strength? He kicked in a door; what if we made the door heavy? Few doors on houses are made of steel or other metals, but how about this: *John kicked in the mahogany door, stormed up the stairs, slapped Maria, and hurled Joaquin through a window.* Is the scene a little more descriptive now? You could have written ". . . heavy mahogany door . . ." but *heavy* and *mahogany* would almost be redundant. Since we get a sense of weight from *mahogany* without writing *heavy*, we can avoid using the more common adjective.

Split Infinitives and Other Non-Problems

Hey, we're talking about the nuances of the language here and how what you've written is going to affect your reader. An infinitive is a verb with the **preposition** *to* in front of it: to go, to ride, to stay, to bark, to complain, to laugh, etc. A split infinitive is that combination interrupted by an adverb: to quickly go, to slowly ride, to gruffly bark, to permanently stay, to loudly complain, to finally laugh, etc. Sometimes the use of these is not a good idea and sometimes (gasp!) it is. Everything depends on the sense the writer is trying to convey.

Author Bernard Shaw once wrote a letter of complaint to *The London Times*. It read, in part,

> "There is a busy body on your staff who devotes a lot of his time to chasing split infinitives. Every good literary craftsman splits his infinitive when the sense demands it. I call for the immediate dismissal of this pedant. It is of no consequence whether he

decides to go quickly or to quickly go. The important thing is that he should go at once."

If it's good enough for Bernard Shaw, it's good enough for me. Besides, as I mention throughout this book, everything you put on the page should be placed with a thought for how it will affect the reader and/or how the reader will react. All other considerations are secondary.

Using Narrative Instead of Dialogue

In a work that is peopled with characters who communicate at all, it is seldom necessary, and almost never advisable, to convey information to the reader through the use of lengthy narrative passages. Very often this practice leads to simply telling the reader what's going on rather than painting a quick picture for him as a context for dialogue or allowing the characters to paint the picture for him. If a narrative passage is unnecessary, omit it. For more on this, see Chapter 4.

That having been said, I've seen some excellent stories written almost entirely in narrative. In most of those stories, though, the narrative is quasi-dialogue or, more precisely, quasi-monologue. The narrator relates his story directly to the reader, as if both are hunched over a table in the corner of a neighborhood bar. The reader listens intently because he is directly engaged as a character by the narrator. When the narrative is well written, the reader quickly and happily assumes the role of the unseen character. One example of this kind of narrative is my own short story, "Soft as a Breeze," which you can view on my website at http://stonethread.com. The story is about the narrator's friend, Jimmy, whose nickname you'll remember is Digger, and the setting is a combat zone:

> Being there was mostly boring. Long periods of nothin' to do but wait for somethin' to happen. It was quiet and soft and sweet, a lot like Jimmy, 'til that one scalding, blinding-white instant when all hell breaks loose and then is reconfined. All

in that split second. I mean there's a big lead-up that's sort of excitin' and scary and lasts longer than time when things are happening all around you and you're diving for a hole and grabbing your rifle and trying to stick a magazine in upside down and throwing ammo to your buddy and dodging sounds all at once, kind of like a spooked house cat. But it's still okay 'cause it ain't happening directly *to* you.

Then there's that scalding-hot second of pure hell when the whole damn mess centers on you, just you, when you're all by yourself and so is your buddy who's only a foot away, when you think the earth is spitting little puffs of dirt at you 'til an eternity-long split second later when you remember it's bullets, when all the rain in every drizzly, miserable cloud on earth is falling within a two-foot radius of the center of your head and everything and everyone is screaming at you or past you and you can't do anything as fast or as good as you have every day of your life like duck or run or get out of the mud or find a trigger or remember a friend who pulled you out of a tunnel two weeks ago, then — then the instant ends and you're alive. And you've got to get capable again.

You start to stop shaking and you think of a cigarette and reach for one, then Mom flashes a disapproving look through your mind, but you reach anyway, then you want to joke with your friend, show him you're both still bad, tell him Charlie'd rather sandpaper a bear's ass in a phone booth than mess with you and he smiles kind of soft in your mind and you want to offer to split that extra beer in your pack with him, you know? *Split a beer with the wind* you think maybe help *his* nerves a little bit and you smile, so you think to reach for it but decide to joke first and get the beer in a second and you're smiling and turning your head and opening your mouth to tell him about bear's asses in phone booths —

But his face is gone.

Then your body is turning inside out and you can't hear and all you feel is screaming and scalding water on your cheeks even in the rain that's too damn hard and cold and miserable to care about anything and four guys jump on you like the rain and the wind, hard like thugs, take your breath like a gale like a damn firestorm, not soft not like a breeze and they yell things like *Shhh!* and *Shut up!* and they use your name like they know you but you scream right through their hands right through the blood and bones grimy meat of their filthy, muddy, bony fucking hands. Screaming.

Screaming for a breeze, just a soft little breeze. But the breeze is gone.

The louie came up the next day with his head down. Said how Digger took a round to the side of his head, how it looked like it hit his right cheekbone. And he said how he was real sorry, not because he *had* to, like some lieutenants, but because he really was sorry. But he had nothin' to be sorry for. Hell, I mean, even Jimmy wasn't soft enough there, you know? Nobody is.

The best, most effective writing happens as a result of the writer's awareness and use of the nuances of the language. Those nuances are the sounds of letters and words, the length of sentences, and the punctuation used. The writer must be as aware of those nuances to write great narrative just as he must to write great dialogue. And whereas dialogue almost always is necessary because it's being spoken by characters about a situation in the story, with narrative, the writer has the additional albatross of having constantly to decide whether the narrative he's been working on for three hours is necessary at all. It might be truly great writing in and of itself, yet be a hindrance to the story rather than an asset. But all that aside for the moment, given that the narrative is necessary to the story line, the great writer must manipulate words, phrases, sentences, and punctuation in such a way that the reader will *sense* that she's reading something she doesn't want to put down. She won't know why, but that's all right. That's the magic of a really good book.

Of course, as with any good tool, it's possible to carry the use of narrative too far. In Chapter 4, we'll explore that and other overuses that can put a crimp in your readership.

Summary

Narrative can be used as an adjunct to dialogue by the use of tag lines and brief introductory or interruptive descriptive narratives or as quasi-dialogue (monologue) when the story will be more effective if related directly to the reader. Once we use a noun to put a picture into the reader's mind, we use an action verb to make the picture move. Our use of action verbs reduces our use of the passive voice and our dependence on descriptive adjectives and adverbs. The combination of these attributes of narrative creates a powerful tool the writer can use to more quickly and thoroughly suspend the reader's disbelief.

Chapter 4   How to Lose a Reader

Until now, this book has focused on what you should do as a writer to keep the reader reading, to avoid interrupting her. After all, when she's completely absorbed in reading your novel, so into it that her boyfriend has to say her name three times before she even realizes he's in the room, why would you want to do something to interrupt her? The short answer is you wouldn't.

But just in case, in this chapter I'm going to teach you how to lose a reader. If you really want to live the whole "struggling, starving writer" experience, unable to find a market for your work even after you've received rave reviews from your mom and your uncles and all your siblings except that mean one, just do the things I talk about here.

Unnecessary or Excessive Text

Few problems will cause a reader to grind to a disgusted halt more quickly than will unnecessary narrative. When the narrator talks too much about himself (uses too much "I"); explains too much to the reader rather than allowing the reader to see what's going on; over-describes a character, a situation or scene; or talks down to the reader by beating him over the head with information that practically everybody knows, *he will lose that reader*. Let's look at some of the more prevalent problems.

Unnecessary Tag Lines or Not Enough Tag Lines

For an excellent example of using as few tag lines as possible, read Ernest Hemingway's short story, "Hills Like White Elephants." This might be the only example I've seen of a writer possibly not using enough tag lines. (I say "possibly" because it's difficult to fault Hemingway.) In that story, during the lengthy conversation between the man and girl in the station, the reader might get lost and have to count back several lines to determine who's speaking. On the other hand, most tag line errors come in the form of a deluge. Especially novice writers seem to think they have to write "he said" or "she said" after every bit of dialogue.

Here's my rule of thumb: Use a tag line only when it's absolutely necessary to let the reader know which character is speaking. When the reader can determine which character is speaking from the context of the dialogue or through brief descriptive narrative passages, omit tag lines. If you have to err, err on the side of fewer tag lines rather than more. If nothing else, eliminating tag lines will cause the reader to pay closer attention to the story.

Convoluted Construction

A convoluted construction is one that winds its way through two or three or four levels before returning to the original topic, and in almost every case it will confuse the reader. When the reader gets confused, he'll stop reading until he finds his place again or until he re-reads the text and figures out what's going on. Unless he's tired of being confused by your work; in that case, he'll stop reading, period. Remember, any interruption is a bad thing.

Some writers, all novices as far as I can tell, actually believe the convoluted construction is a good thing, that a reader should have to work to understand their meaning. Apparently these are graduates of the same ivory-tower school of extremely light knocks whence come the intellectuals who believe good poetry must be mystical, obscure, or otherwise difficult to understand. Such a belief is pure, unadulterated bull cookies. The reader is doing you a favor. She pays good money to be informed or entertained by you, and she shouldn't have to "interpret" your meaning. Only lawyers intentionally write things that have to be interpreted, and that's so people like you and I have to hire them to interpret for us. Otherwise, they and their brethren would have no place to report for work tomorrow. But I digress.

Although convolution usually occurs in a sentence or paragraph of dialogue or narrative, I had to title this section "Convoluted Construction" because it can occur at any level: sentence, paragraph, essay or story, chapter, or even novel. One novel manuscript I edited hooked me immediately with strong action, but soon afterward the author dropped me into a flashback, then another, then another, and on back. These weren't separate flashbacks from the present; it was from the present to the first flashback, from that one to the second, then the third, and so on. And while in the third or fourth flashback, the scene shifted from one dynastic family to another and from one country to another. If a *flashback* is intended to transport the reader back in time, I suppose the last couple of shifts would have to be called *flashsides* or *flashlaterals*. Anyway, by that time, I was so confused I couldn't remember the protagonist's name. You'll see a more in-depth discussion of this particular mess later in this chapter. Also, you'll find several other examples of convoluted construction in different sections throughout this chapter.

Lengthy Look-At-Me Paragraphs

Ever been in a social gathering where one person dominates the conversation? And as if that weren't bad enough, the conversation is all about "I" and "me"? Everything the person says somehow relates back to herself. In a book, few things are more distracting and annoying than look-at-me passages of narrative. They seldom, if ever, actually contribute to the story line and probably are the primary cause of novels being hurled through plate-glass windows.

The look-at-me narrative passage is most often about the author himself, but also can be about the main character. It's most often written in first person by the narrator, whether author or character, and usually contains a flood of completely unnecessary, boring information. Furthermore, it takes the form of a particularly annoying text block (it's no longer words and sentences, but a garbled mass) that the reader, after the first couple of times, will learn to avoid by skipping it in its entirety — if the book otherwise is interesting enough to justify the reader working that hard to stay involved. In every case, the narrator happily supplies the look-at-me narrative because he sees himself as so special and interesting that surely the reader will be interested. In every case, the narrator is wrong.

If the self-serving narrative passage also serves to further the story line or provide necessary clarity for the reader, and if it isn't lengthy, it's a good thing. If it's too long, no matter how well written, it will prove a distraction to the reader. In an, intelligent, novel-length manuscript titled *The Search for Gojesmo*, Mac Fallows, an excellent young musician and writer from Canada, absolutely enthralled me with strong, interesting dialogue; witty, brief, engaging narrative; and a story line that was so good it was almost unfair. The reader who encounters anything Mr. Fallows has written simply has no choice but to enjoy it.

When I edited the manuscript for him, Mr. Fallows asked me specifically to be sure to mention any content problems I might stumble across. I found only one. From near the end of page 5 through the end of page 9, the narrator narrated . . . and narrated . . . and . . . well, you get the idea. Now, unlike most lengthy narrative passages in most manuscripts, this particular narrative actually was important to the story line. It was also interesting, but it *starkly interrupted the wonderful rhythm of the story*, which Mr. Fallows himself had established and which had otherwise balanced almost perfectly between dialogue and narrative, for four pages. What's worse, the narrator's personal "I" occurred 99 times in just over four pages. (Actually, it occurred 101 times, but two of those were in the titles of songs he'd written during his childhood.) That's an average of 24 occurrences per page, and remember, none of these were used in dialogue (i.e., "I can't go"). In the rest of the manuscript, in narrative, dialogue, and song lyrics, the personal "I" occurred an average of 15 times per page. Quite a difference.

Because the narrative itself was important to the story line, I suggested he keep most of it, but break it up with remembered dialogue — for example, an exchange that occurred in his presence between his parents and his high school guidance counselor.

As I've mentioned, the lengthy narrative passage is seldom important to the story, or to anything else, for that matter, besides the narrator's ego. Not only is it usually excessive, but when it becomes lengthy, it also often becomes unwieldy and tends to wander off-subject. Worse, it creates not only an interruption, but a massive interruption, one from which the relationship between your book and your reader might well not recover.

Narrative Passages That Have Nothing to Do With the Plot

Fiction, at its most basic, is the suspension of a reader's disbelief. Because the reader is no fool and realizes that fiction is not the same thing as reality, that suspension is easy to come by — after all, the reader graciously suspends his own disbelief — but maintaining that suspension is another matter altogether. That's your job. The reader enters into an unspoken contract with you. In return for his belief in your world, you implicitly agree not to burst his bubble. You agree to allow him to escape his own reality for as long as he wants or until your story or book ends, whichever happens sooner.

The reader also is an understanding, forgiving person who really wants to be in your fictional world — after all, he bought the book — so he's more than willing to overlook the occasional screw up, especially if it's humorous, as are (for example) most misplaced modifiers. But under no circumstances will he allow you to bore him with a bunch of fluff that has nothing to do with the characters or the **plot** or the scene.

Here's the example from that novel-length manuscript I mentioned earlier: You'll remember that the author, after hooking me with an excellent beginning in the midst of hot, intriguing action, unexpectedly inserted a flashback, then another and another *ad nauseam.* Why? Because he wanted to convince me that the protagonist was indeed qualified to be in a covert aircraft over a Latin American country and to explain in detail why that protagonist was about to parachute, under cover of darkness, into the stronghold of a drug lord.

Understand, these are flashbacks within flashbacks within flashbacks. For future reference, I'll tell you that the flashbacks, in descending order, went from the present-day protagonist in the covert aircraft back to when he'd first become interested in skydiving, then to his days as an ambulance driver, then to a really bad accident he worked as an ambulance driver, then to how the hospital administration set up the shifts at the hospital for which he worked as an ambulance driver, then — well, you probably get the idea. And as I mentioned earlier, in one or two of those flashbacks he sidestepped into another part of the world and a whole new cast of characters (the chief antagonist's relatives and ancestors), while still in the past, to club me with what seemed like the endlessly convoluted circumstances that had led the antagonists to *their* current situation. I felt as if I were reading at least three novels simultaneously: a romance, a thriller, and a family saga ala Michener's *Texas.*

Now, I have to tell you that I had absolutely *no* interest in the life experiences that eventually caused the protagonist to be perched at the open hatch of an aircraft, poised to parachute into a hostile stronghold. Even as the editor of the manuscript, I made the natural, readerly assumption that the protagonist was qualified to be the protagonist. If he weren't qualified, well, I assume the writer would have fired him and gotten himself a new protagonist. But the point is this: As a reader, I shouldn't be led to think about any of those things in the first place.

Let me be as clear as I can be: Specifically *because* the reader so willingly and graciously suspends his own disbelief, it is among the chief traits of fiction that the writer doesn't *have* to explain whether his protagonist is qualified to *be* the protagonist. As part of their willing suspension of disbelief, readers simply assume all is well in the fictional world in which they're about to vacation. Please, don't run them off.

Here's a fictional example of a convoluted narrative passage that has nothing to do with the story line. A lawyer is addressing a juvenile court judge on behalf of his charge:

> "This boy's mother and grandmother were both killed in the big flood, Your Honor." That was all the attorney had to say. The judge knew he was referring to the great flood of 1973, which was caused by Hurricane Gilbert and had killed 5,000 people. The lawyer knew Hurricane Gilbert had loitered in the Atlantic for several days, building in strength because his cousin worked for the weather service. He hadn't slept in all those days before the hurricane hit, but afterward he slept like a baby. "He's lived on the streets ever since, supporting himself in any way he could. He's not a criminal; he's just never had a break."

Since the lawyer referred to the event as "the big flood," won't the reader probably assume everyone present is familiar with that event? So explaining what the judge knew not only is redundant, irritating, and unnecessary, but that information has no direct bearing on the story line. The lawyer's contention is that boy was on the street because his mother and grandmother were killed; how they were killed doesn't matter in the slightest. "That was all the attorney had to say" also is unnecessary. And what possible relevance does the lawyer's cousin or his profession or his sleeping habits have to the proceedings? Just so you know, neither the cousin nor the weather service nor any of the lawyer's personal habits were mentioned ever again.

To clean up this passage, let simply remove all the narrative. In doing so, do we deprive the reader of anything?

"This boy's mother and grandmother were both killed in the big flood, Your Honor. He's lived on the streets ever since, supporting himself in any way he could. He's not a criminal, Your Honor; he's just never had a break."

If someone asked me how I came to write this book on dialogue and flash fiction, I wouldn't begin by telling them about the day I tripped over a curb and ripped the knee out of my new jeans, or the time I nearly electrocuted myself (my dad said) by trying to pry a bird's nest out of an electrical box with a stick while standing in a puddle of rainwater, or the evening I first discovered girls were not just soft boys. Those memories certainly are relevant to my own life, but none of them has anything to do with my being a writer now.

Beating the Reader Over the Head

One of the most difficult things for the writer to do is *trust the reader to get it*, whatever "it" might be. I've found that readers generally know pretty much everything that I know about the world. In the rough manuscript for a crime drama, you might read something like this:

"The perp, short for perpetrator, which is what we call a suspected criminal, fled along the sidewalk. Casting a sidelong glance over his shoulder, he flipped over a fire hydrant, one of those red spark-plug-looking things scattered around the city for emergency use by the fire department when they need water, and landed squarely in the ninety degree angle formed by a light pole and the curb. He lay moaning and holding his right thigh. He could easily have broken his leg when he hit the fire hydrant."

The problem, of course, is that most readers already know what *perp* means, what a fire hydrant looks like and its purpose, that a light pole intersecting a curb forms a ninety degree angle, and that the guy might have broken his leg when he hit the fire hydrant. Repeating all this information indicates that you don't trust the reader to know these things, and it will cost you sales. With any luck at all, by the time the manuscript is a book on the shelf, the passage will read something like this:

> "The perp fled along the sidewalk. Casting a sidelong glance over his shoulder, he flipped over a fire hydrant and landed squarely in the angle of a light pole and the curb. He lay moaning and holding his right thigh."

Sometimes narrative is excessive but not blatant. Let's return to the lawyer/judge example of the previous section for a moment. The narrative here is subtle enough, but is it necessary or excessive?

> Intrigued by the attorney's defense, the judge contemplated what he'd heard. "I see. . . . Are you willing to take him in and accept responsibility for him?"

Think about this passage for a moment. *Of course* the judge contemplated what he'd heard; after all, he's a judge in a courtroom listening to a lawyer — that's his job. And when the judge says "I see" (especially since it's followed by an ellipsis), he indicates both that he's intrigued and that he's contemplating what he's been told. That's why we don't need this descriptive narrative. This example is a little more subtle, but it's still beating the reader over the head.

Here's another example of a writer both providing unnecessary information and beating him over the head with information that most people already know:

> "Unit five-oh, what's your twenty?" came the call from the dispatcher. John and his partner were in unit 50 that day referred to as "five-oh."
> Their "twenty" (location and status) was William Beaumont Army Medical Center, having just delivered an automobile accident victim.

Instead of explaining that "five-oh" is another way of saying "fifty" and giving the reader the definition of "twenty" and then explaining where they were and what they were doing, the narrator should delete the unnecessary information and let the character speak for himself, especially since another character (the dispatcher) had asked him a direct question:

> The radio squawked. "Unit five-oh, what's your twenty?"
> John keyed the mike. "Just arrived at Beaumont, dropping one."

Most readers would know that "Unit 50" would be pronounced "Unit five-oh" (and what difference would it make anyway?) and most readers would know that "twenty" (10-20 in Ten Code) means location and status. Plus, those who *didn't* know what "twenty" meant could easily figure it out from the context of the dispatcher's question and John's response. Notice that in the revised example, we also said just "Beaumont" and referred to "dropping one." We assume the dispatcher, who probably sent John on the run in the first place, would know he'd worked a traffic accident, and that "dropping one" would mean "one victim," especially since they're dropping one at Beaumont, a hospital.

Another variation of beating the reader over the head with information occurs when the narrator overuses a character's name instead of occasionally (and appropriately) substituting a pronoun or other key identifier. Although this most often happens in tag lines, it also sometimes happens in narrative passages. *Overuse of the characters' names in a narrative passage often indicates that the information in the narrative passage would be more economically delivered through dialogue.* Consider this fictional example:

> Safely back inside the Silverado, Paul and John shivered with cold. Paul wrestled with the keys for a moment and finally found the ignition key. He started the truck and the engine roared to life. Paul reached to adjust the heater to its

highest setting. John asked Paul what they were going to do next. Paul told John he wasn't sure, but that they surely couldn't stay there. John agreed. Paul clapped him on the shoulder and told him they'd be all right. John forced a smile and said he'd be glad when they saw the lights of the city again.

Some narrative is necessary here to set the scene, but most of this could have been related through dialogue between Paul and John:

> Safely back inside the Silverado, the two men shivered with cold. Paul wrestled with the keys for a moment, then started the engine. He turned on the heater.
> John looked at him. "So what now?"
> "I don't know. We sure can't stay around here."
> "Yeah. It's . . . ."
> "Hey." Paul clapped him on the shoulder. "Everything's gonna be fine."
> "Yeah. Well, I'll just be glad when we see the lights of Detroit."
> "You and me both, Brother."

Is the second example more interesting than the first? You'll notice that in the second example, we initially refer to John and Paul as "the two men." This allows the reader to learn their names on his own, as if by accident rather than being told outright. Notice too that we use Paul's name only twice and John's only once, yet there's no confusion regarding which one is talking.

Misplaced Modifiers

These are the little reversals that almost always cause a laugh. Still, they pull your reader from the story line and should be avoided. The good news is that readers tend to think we misplace modifiers on purpose to get a laugh, so most of the time they keep reading, though maybe not for the reason you'd prefer. Take a look at these examples and the correct versions below them.

Wrong: Walking into the clubhouse, the cement floor was littered with helmets, mouth pieces, girdles, pads, and protection cups but no coffee container.

(No way did the cement floor walk into that clubhouse.)

Corrected: They walked into the clubhouse. The cement floor was littered with helmets, mouth pieces, girdles, pads, and protective cups, but there was no coffee container.

Wrong: Looking at each other, Buck replied.

(I can almost guarantee you that Buck cannot look at each other.)

Corrected: As they looked at each other, Buck replied.

Wrong: Crossing over the Harlem River and entering Manhattan Island, the buildings became taller. With each passing block the wealth increased and I kept thinking, for what purpose.

(Nope. The buildings definitely did *not* cross the Harlem River. When I first read this, my initial reaction was, *Yes, for what purpose do you keep thinking?*)

Corrected: We crossed the Harlem River to Manhattan Island, where the buildings were taller and signs of affluence increased with each passing block.

Wrong: After showering and while shaving my telephone rang.

(I'd bet the telephone did not shower and shave.)

Corrected: After I'd showered and while I was shaving, my telephone rang.

Wrong: Ralph's head popped up from the menu stating to everyone . . . .

(Ralph's head probably is on Ralph's shoulders, not in the menu.)

Corrected: Browsing the menu, Ralph looked up.

And finally, a few of my favorites from a college English class:

Wrong: My mother feeds chocolates to her friends with soft centers.

(Some of her mother's friends have soft centers?)

Corrected: My mother feeds her friends chocolates with soft centers.

Wrong: Riding his bicycle, a dog bit Roy.

(Most dogs don't ride bicycles.)

Corrected: A dog bit Roy as he rode his bicycle.

Wrong: Susan hung out the clothes wringing wet.

(Susan probably was not wringing wet.)

Corrected: Susan hung out the wet clothes.

Inanity

These snippets usually occur as a result of the writer's mind wandering. Actually, I can't come up with a legitimate reason for these or even a good excuse for them unless you're writing a story like *Rainman*. The narrative is moving along just fine when, for no apparent reason, it goes off the deep end. Check out these examples from novels I've edited. Any minor repairs I made to them are enclosed in brackets:

> Suddenly, John couldn't help but think of DEA Agent Ernesto Carrera. 'Neto had been kidnapped and tortured to death by some dope smugglers in Mexico over the loss of few hundred-thousand dollars worth of marijuana. The Honduran drug lord they were about to challenge was capable of much harsher treatment. John's final question, spoken softly to himself was, *Where am I going to find a case of beer in Honduras?*

Wait a minute — the guy is worried about where he's going to find a case of beer? And while we're at it, what's your definition of "much harsher treatment" than kidnapping and torture?

> The white, red and blue ambulance with its flashing strings of red, blue and white lights strung across its roof, down its sides, and crisscrossing the rear door, roared off carrying poor Fish's remains like a berserk Christmas tree fleeing the woodsman's ax.

There's too much description here *and* a messed-up simile. Anybody else get a mental picture of a Christmas tree with legs? Gotta watch out for those berserk Christmas trees.

> On the screen, a sort of black news reader guy who wasn't all that black, sort of coffee ice cream tan whose top hair was black and side hair gray with glasses atop a nose job and posed a somber demean, had started to read off a TelePrompTer that new revelations in the growing scandal involving Albany and New York City charities, have just unfolded.

There's too much description here and this one is just a bit convoluted, isn't it? The writer got wrapped around the wheel trying to describe the appearance of the "news reader guy." I'm not sure what he meant by "posed a somber demean" unless he meant "posing with a somber demeanor." I suggested he recast the paragraph.

She sounded surprised to hear from me, and deciding to gloss over the fact I had only a few, well no other alternative, [I told] her my call was motivated by my deep love for her, the same desperate wild love that forces a man to give up all for the woman he loves.

There's too much description here and, again, a bit of convolution. Why does the writer give us so much unnecessary detail? Your guess is as good as any.

One peek into the huge dark room where multi-colored lights threw iridescent confetti across the dark spaces, and flashes of laser lightning criss-crossed a cavernous room filled with [the] ear deadening, soul frightening roar of hundreds of people screaming, bouncing and gyrating as a heavy metal band called "Vomit" yelling from amplifiers, "Baby we want it all . . . all . . . all," over and over again, took all the Pilgrims' Thanksgiving spirit out of the choir.

There's far too much description here. The only bright point is the stark contrast between the raucous racket described through most of the paragraph and the mental image of a choir witnessing it. That renders it humorous enough to make the whole scene almost worthwhile.

I was at rest on the couch in the peaceful time between our brisk late morning walks, our brunches of pancakes and eggs with hot coffee, and the late evening's dark quiet, punctuated only by the sound of the fire burping air from eating the log's sap, and the sound of the night wind saying 'hello,' as it passed by.

Again, there's too much description. And between "the fire burping air from eating the log's sap" and "the sound of the night wind saying 'hello,' as it passed by," it was all I could do not to roll out of my chair and onto the floor laughing.

I imagine a lot of you are looking at these examples and thinking, *Yeah, but the reader would know what we meant to say.* That might be true, but the point is that such slips of the mind create a diversion that pulls the reader from the story line. And if you're thinking *Well, these are the kinds of things the editor will fix,* again, that might be true in a few cases, but I don't know an editor at any publishing house, major or otherwise, who would continue even to read a manuscript with such problems, much less accept it for publication and spend time repairing it. In fact, a lot of freelance editors won't work on such a manuscript, or they'll charge you extra to suggest fixes for problems like these.

In my own freelance editing endeavors, I offer a free sample edit that allows the writer to see my editing ability and style and allows me to see the writer's style. I no longer accept manuscripts with problems like the ones above, though I still provide the free sample edit and am happy to refer them to some of my freelancing colleagues. For information, visit http://stonethread.com.

Erroneous Facts

Few problems irritate a reader as much as stumbling across an outright lie that indicates ignorance on the part of the writer. As I mentioned before, the author and reader are under contract to each other. The writer creates a fictional world, populates it, and establishes a set of rules by which the fictional characters are bound. The reader suspends disbelief, allowing the writer the rules of his fictional world. For example, we all know humans can't defy gravity without the aid of balloons or machines, but if one humanoid being *can* fly in the writer's fictional world because he came to Earth from a planet with two red suns, we don't give it a second thought. As long as the writer and the characters live within the rules of the fictional world, everything's fine. But most fictions contain at least some references to the real world in which we live, and that's where some writers run into problems.

You can have your super-human being flying around the planet saving lives and helping his charges avert catastrophe after catastrophe, but if he teams up with a unit of Navy SEALS, don't say about one of the SEALS that "he was an expert at SNA — silent neutralization of the enemy" because there is no such acronym, and anyone who has much military experience knows it. And don't have the "extras" in your novel harvesting sugar cane to make mescal because mescal is distilled from the agave plant, not from sugar cane.

Each of Louis L'Amour's western novels contained a statement all writers should live by: Paraphrased, the statement reads *When Louis L'Amour writes about a stream, the stream is there and the water is good to drink.* Another way to say it is *Do your research.*

The Infamous *Gave*

When I happen across the first couple of instances of an inappropriate use of "gave" in a manuscript, I immediately do a global search to find each instance all the way through. I find that when I've discovered one "gave," I'll no doubt discover a lot more of them. Using "gave" inappropriately creates the same kind of diversion as someone who says "umm" a lot during the course of a speech. After a while, the audience members stop listening to the speech and start counting occurrences of "umm." Likewise, the reader will begin wondering when you're going to quit "giving" things that can't be given. Here's a verbatim transcript of a question/answer session between a writer and his editor (me):

Question: Which sentence is correct or are they both correct?

"I gave a quick look at Nick Campbell, and he gave me a subtle nod for me to continue."

"I gave a quick look at Nick Campell, and he gave me a subtle nod to continue."

A: I don't care for either of them. In the first place, "give" is most often a transitive verb, meaning you actually give (or hand or grant) something to someone. Using it as you use it in these sentences is all right if it isn't overused; however, when a writer uses it in this way, he most often overuses it. Regarding the problem you're actually wondering about, whether the "nod to continue" phrase works, it really doesn't. To fix both problems (verb and phrase), I'd recommend writing it like this:

"I glanced at Nick Campbell and he nodded, indicating I should continue."

"Glanced" is an action verb that indicates "quickly looked" without having to write "quickly." He didn't actually "nod to continue" or "nod for me to continue," but his nod indicated that Nick should continue.

When you "give" someone a nod or a smile or a look or a glance or whatever, that indicates to the reader that the recipient has something now that she didn't have before, as if you "gave" her a dollar or ring or a house or some writing advice.

So here's the thing — if you're one of those writers who bathes in "gave," stop it. If you look at the third or fourth word after "gave," most often it will be a noun (smile, wave, shake) that you can turn into a past-tense verb (smiled, waved, shook) and use in place of *gave*.

Don't Write	Write
"I gave him a smile."	"I smiled (at him)."

"I gave him a wave."	"I waved (to him)."
"I gave his hand a shake."	"I shook his hand."
"I gave her a kiss."	"I kissed her."

however . . .

Please Write	Not
"I gave him a dollar."	"I dollared him."
"I gave her a ring."	"I ringed (rang?) her."

Yeah, I know you didn't need the last couple of lines of instruction, but we're about to discuss a little grammar, so I thought you deserved this minor respite.

State-of-Being Verbs

If you know anything about writing anything other than term papers or instructional manuals, you know to avoid the state-of-being verbs unless you're intentionally describing a state of being. State-of-being verbs are the cornerstone of the passive voice; effective fiction and creative nonfiction is written in the active voice.

For reference, the state-of-being verbs are *am, is, are, was, were, be, being,* and *been.* Way back in "Using Action Verbs to Create a Mental Movie" in Chapter 3, I used my favorite example. It will suffice here as well:

"John was angry."

Do you get any sense of John or what's going on in the scene from that sentence?

"John was very, very, very angry."

Does the addition of the repeated *very* help? Do you know any more now about the scene than you knew a moment ago?

"John's face was red; he was excruciatingly angry."

How about now? Nope. The first *was* simply tells (not shows) the reader the color of John's face, and the second one describes John's state-of-being. Rather than letting the reader see John — rather than letting John's actions show the reader John is angry — we just keep trying to up the ante with state-of-being verbs, adjectives and adverbs.

Let's try one more time:

"John kicked in the door, stormed up the stairs, slapped Maria, and hurled Joaquin through a window."

Ah, now you see what's going on in the scene! The action verbs — *kicked, stormed, slapped,* and *hurled* — provide us with a mental movie. Always remember that anytime you use a state-of-being verb, you're telling the reader something rather than letting him see it for himself.

Summary

We've learned that unnecessary or excessive text, whether in the form of tag lines, convoluted constructions, look-at-me narrative, or mis-placed modifiers, will pull the reader from the fictional world in which he's invested his time and money. We also know to trust the reader rather than explaining things that pretty much everyone already knows. We know it's better to be sure of our facts rather than winging it, and that we should avoid using "gave" inappropriately or using state-of-being verbs at any time. Why do these things matter? Because they interrupt the reader, and when you've interrupted him once too many times, you've lost him.

Chapter 5   Writing Flash Fiction

To say that writing good fiction is difficult is among the worst of understatements. Writing good fiction within the confines of the short-short story (various sources place the length restriction at 500, 1000, 1500, and 2000 words) is much more difficult. To attempt the same feat in fewer than 100 words is insanity. But when the tools of therapy include paper and a pen, insanity isn't necessarily a bad thing.

Proponents, contest administrators, and publishers of flash fiction place length restrictions variously up to 500 or even 1,000 words, but one of the largest markets restricts the form to 55 words (not including the title, which should not exceed five words). For our purposes, flash fiction is a complete story — one with a beginning, a middle, and an end — written in 99 words or fewer not including the title. Flash fiction often has a surprise ending, a twist delivered in the last line or two, because it provides a final impact; however, a surprise ending is not a requirement.

Flash Fiction Defined

Although flash fiction is extremely short, it retains all of the primary components of a complete story: *setting, characters,* and *conflict,* all of which lead, finally, to the *resolution,* which should effect a change.

You probably noticed that I didn't mention *plot* as a separate component; *plot* is a series of causal events (conflicts) leading eventually to the resolution of the story. Since, in this format, there is no room for a series of anything, *plot* must necessarily be considered less important and, at best, occurring in the reader's mind as a result of implication. More on this later. You cannot tell a story, though, *without* setting, characters, conflict, and resolution, so these requirements are not unique to flash fiction.

Notice that this form is real fiction and is not simply an essay or vignette or prose poem or story premise. An old saw regarding fiction teaches us to introduce a character, put him up a tree, throw rocks at him, and bring him down. Be wary of writing only part of a story, in which the character is stranded in the tree. Let's look at a few forms that are similar to flash fiction at first glance.

Genres That Are Not Flash Fiction

Essay

The essayist strives primarily to define a topic, argue a point and convince you he's right, issue a call to arms, or entertain you. When the essayist entertains, he most often does so with satire or outright, curmudgeonly sarcasm. Essays written primarily to evoke humor, like those of Erma Bombeck, border the slice of life or vignette. No matter its purpose, every well-written essay has a beginning, a middle, and an end. In that way, at least, it resembles fiction. But an essayist seldom establishes conflict except to establish her point in the context of argument, and without conflict there can be no resolution. Also, although some essays include characters, usually the narrator and an antagonist, characters are not required.

Vignette (Slice of Life)

The vignette or slice of life is a fictional account. If a short story is a film, the vignette is a snapshot. Imagine you are walking along a sidewalk that abuts a large apartment building. As you near an open window, the voices of two people inside the apartment begin to come into range. If you write what you overhear from then until the voices fade out as you pass by the window and move farther away, you have written a vignette, a small, thin slice of the life of the people in that apartment.

The vignette includes a setting and characters, and most often it includes a conflict, but it never includes a resolution. For that reason, it is a slice of life, not the whole pie.

Prose Poem

In a so-called prose poem, the emphasis is on imagery, not character, conflict, setting, or resolution. In the worst of these, the writer strings together a succession of errant, disconnected thoughts, a list that neither tells a story nor provides the reader with anything more than, confusing, disjointed imagery. In the best of what has been presented to me as a prose poem, I've discovered a vignette, albeit a delightful one, both beautifully written and full of vivid imagery.

My point is this: If it doesn't have 14 lines, it might be a beautiful poem, but it isn't a sonnet. If it doesn't have a setting, characters, at least one conflict, and a satisfactory resolution, it isn't a story, flash fiction or otherwise.

Story Premise

The story premise, obviously, is not a genre, but I included it here because I've seen some folks confuse a flash fiction story for a premise. Although you can use a flash fiction story as a basis from which to launch a longer story — one of my friends turned a flash fiction story into an award-winning novella — it is much more than a premise. The story premise contains none of the elements of fiction; it only hints at them. Most often, the story premise is framed in the form of a question that begins What if?

For example, *What if a jealous husband suspects his wife of cheating on him with a priest?* is a premise. In this case, the premise provides the characters. Building on that premise to include a conflict and a satisfactory resolution makes the premise a story.

The Elements of Flash Fiction

As I've already mentioned a couple of times, a complete short story has four distinct elements: setting, characters, conflict, and resolution. Flash fiction has a fifth element that is more necessary than in other forms of creative writing: suggestion. Let's look at some definitions.

Setting

The setting is simply the locale wherein the characters act out the scene(s) and the events or occurrences take place, whether a universe, a solar system, a world, an ocean, a country, a state, a forest, a field, a town, a house, a car, a tea cup, a painting, or the character's mind. You needn't worry too much about coming up with a setting. It's all but impossible to begin a story without a setting occurring naturally.

Characters

Characters are players in the story, but the writer needn't limit his characters to human beings. They might be human, of course, but they might also be animal, vegetable, mineral, mechanical, or alien. When we think of a player in a story, we often think of the character who delivers a line of dialogue or who delivers action through narrative, but the recipient of the dialogue or action is a player, a character, as well. Even a cotton ball could be a character. For example, *What if Margot, dissatisfied with her marriage, discusses that dissatisfaction with a cotton ball while applying her makeup?* Whether the cotton ball responds depends on the writer and Margot's state of mind, but that is irrelevant. Either way, the cotton ball is a character.

Most flash fiction stories have only one or two characters, and three probably is the limit. You could have several thousand people in a mob, but they would not be characters themselves; they would be component *parts* of the character, the mob, just as an arm or leg or head is a component part of a human character.

Conflict

Conflict is the source of tension that keeps the reader interested in the story, that keeps him wondering what will happen next to the protagonist, the antagonist, or both. Conflict is arguably the most important component of fiction: *Conflict begs resolution.* When we introduce a problem (conflict), the reader wants us also to provide the solution (resolution). You can find many excellent ideas in Chapter 2 and elsewhere in this book for introducing conflict and building tension.

Resolution

Resolution is the natural, satisfactory outcome of the conflict. The key word here is "satisfactory." As is the case with longer works of fiction, the flash-fiction writer must not save the protagonist or otherwise resolve the conflict through miraculous means. That is, as I've mentioned elsewhere in this book, the writer must live within the rules he established for his fictional world.

If the fictional world in which your story takes place is populated with dragons, having a "good" dragon pluck your protagonist from mid-air just after he plunges over a cliff might work. The reader already has accepted that there are dragons in your fictional world, so this resolution would not seem miraculous. But if your protagonist has been established as a typical human being with typical human traits, you can't have him suddenly sprout wings and defy gravity when there's been no previous hint of wing-sprouting, gravity-defying humans.

As you'll see shortly, many flash fiction stories have a surprise or twist ending, but the reader must immediately recognize that the resolution "fits," that it is not only a plausible outcome, but a likely one. The best resolution is one that makes the reader slap himself across the forehead and say "Why didn't I think of that!" It's completely plausible, but also completely unexpected.

Suggestion

Suggestion (or implication) is the fine art of letting the reader know what you're talking about — or letting him think he knows what you're talking about — without telling him directly. If conflict is the most important component of fiction, suggestion is a close second. Most of the emotion conveyed through dialogue and narrative is conveyed through suggestion. When she uses suggestion, the writer hints at an emotion or an occurrence and lets the reader invent it himself rather than telling him about it outright. As you might imagine, suggestion is a valuable tool with many uses. For example, misdirection is an important function of suggestion; you start the reader thinking in one direction, then hit him from another direction. You can find examples of suggestion throughout this book, including a few flash fiction pieces I've included in this chapter.

A Note Regarding Change

In most short stories, novellas, and novels, the protagonist and/or the antagonist experience a change in her personality, her behavior, or her outlook on life. In flash fiction, more often than not, change is more likely to occur not in the character, but in the reader's *perception* of the character or in his perception of the world at large.

The Bones

In various books about writing, we find the phrase "fleshing out the bones," referring to adding form to the structure of a given piece of creative writing. Flash fiction consists of those same bones, very thinly fleshed out with dialogue and narrative and more heavily fleshed out with implication and innuendo.

Word Economy

One of the most difficult things for the writer is to *trust the reader to get it*, to understand what's going on without being told directly. For this reason, we sometimes use more words than are necessary. That's perfectly acceptable in instructional writing — in fact, some wordiness is necessary if the instructional author wants to affect a broader audience — but it's much less desirable in creative writing. Flash fiction, because of its requirement for brevity, is an excellent vehicle for practicing word economy.

Action Verbs, Contractions, Adjectives, and Adverbs

As they pertain to flash fiction, action verbs and contractions are essential; adjectives and adverbs are anathema. Remember, flash fiction is an exercise in word economy. As I mentioned in greater depth in Chapter 3, the more and stronger action verbs you use, the less you'll need or use descriptive adjectives and adverbs.

As you might imagine, when you're counting words, contractions are essential. After all, "haven't" is only one word, whereas "have not" is two. And there's no reason you can't be inventive: "should not have" is three words; "shouldn't have" is two; "shouldn't've" is only one. Remember that when you're truncating "have," it's "'ve" not "of": "should've" not "should of."

For more in-depth information on the use of action verbs and contractions and the lack of adjectives and adverbs, see Chapter 3 of this book. *Punctuation for Writers* also is a strong, friendly resource for grammar issues.

Dialogue Versus Narrative

I've seen some very good flash fiction stories composed of dialogue or mostly composed of dialogue, and I've seen other very good ones composed entirely of narrative. I've also written both myself, usually allowing the story to dictate the form as you will see shortly. As it pertains to word economy, dialogue generally is a more economical vehicle than narrative for delivering suggestion and innuendo. For one thing, as we've seen earlier in this book, dialogue always immediately engages the reader. Having said that, nothing will convince you more strongly one way or the other than your own experimentation.

Flash Fiction as a Tool for Writing Instruction

Because it's an excellent exercise in word economy that's much more difficult than it seems and a lot of fun, flash fiction is a great tool for writing instructors. Because the writer must include all four elements of fiction and compact those elements into such a tight space, Flash Fiction also is a valuable tool for teaching how those elements interact.

What if we have four goldfish named Setting, Characters, Conflict, and Resolution? How well we could watch them interact would depend on the size of the container in which they're swimming. For example, watching the elements of fiction interact in a novel is like trying to watch four goldfish interact in a thousand-gallon tank full of murky water (sub plots, secondary characters, and so on). Watching the same elements interact in a short story is like watching the goldfish interact in a ten-gallon tank. Watching them interact in a flash fiction story is like watching them interact in a gallon jug full of clear water.

Okay, now let's take a look at some goldfish — er, some examples of flash fiction.

Flash Fiction Examples

After each example, I'll discuss the components. Let's consider "At Confession," my own first successful 55-word short story:

At Confession

"Bless me, Father, for I have sinned."
"How long since your last confession?"
"Two years."
"What's the trouble?"
"I have wished death on a man."
"You haven't acted on your wish?"
"Not yet."
"Who is the man?"
"He is cheating with my wife."
The priest paled. "I forgive you."
I shot him through the screen.

In "At Confession," the setting is a confessional. The characters are the first-person narrator and a priest. Notice, first, how you were immediately drawn into the story by the quiet, but tension-filled dialogue. The conflict is complex: At first it takes place in the protagonist's mind (2 years since confession, wishing death on a man), then is transferred to the priest just before the resolution, during which the priest is shot. As an aside, the antagonist in this story is not the priest, but the protagonist's wife, a third character, although she enters the story only through implication.

Notice that implication is also at work coloring the reader's opinion of the priest. The suggestion that the priest is guilty doesn't necessarily justify the harsh resolution, but the priest's implied admission of guilt, first to the reader ("The priest paled"), then to the narrator ("I forgive you") does justify it. We probably would not have been satisfied with the story had we suspected the priest was innocent.

Notice too that the story seems larger than it actually is, seeming to begin before the narrator begins speaking and to continue after the final line. This is a result of an actual plot in this particular story, with the implied first conflict (the wife's infidelity) leading to the second conflict (in the protagonist's mind) leading to the third conflict (the protagonist facing the priest and the priest's ensuing fear) leading to the resolution. Also, we feel satisfied with the ending; what happens to the narrator as a result of his action is of no consequence to us.

As an aside, "At Confession" was turned into a film short. You can view it online by visiting http://stonethread.com and clinking the film link.

Let's look for those same components in a few more examples:

One Way Out

> The sign over the mirror read *One Way Out.*
> "But there is never only one way," Gerard reasoned, and turned away from the sign, reaching for the door through which he had come. It was no longer there.
> Pushing up his sweat-stained ball cap, he massaged his forehead; then, remembering at once the stories of swift Mercury and that mirrors were backed with the stuff, he raced headlong into the mirror, suffering no wounds and sliding safely into home.

Whereas "At Confession" was a real-world mini-drama, "One Way Out" is a stab at surrealism, combining the real world with myth and imagination so that it's difficult to tell with any certainty where myth and imagination end and the real world begins.

There's a lot at work in "One Way Out" for only 79 words. First of all, the sign over the mirror is odd, yet we don't question it, do we? As I mentioned earlier, generally the reader will accept what we give him. Gerard doesn't question the sign either, but the statement on the sign. His reaction perhaps typifies the human reaction to rules. A bit of foreshadowing takes place next, when he adjusts his "ball cap." The human mind, myth, and the physical world mix next, seemingly as the result of his massaging his forehead. Finally, he places faith in his solution, which startles the reader when it works. The story ends with the word "home," perhaps suggesting safety after being lost. You might find other connotations in this and the other stories. That's part of the fun of writing them, or rather, of allowing them to come out.

Let's look at a few more now. From here on out, I'll discuss only one or two major points for each story and let you find the others.

Georgia Peach

"Don't take it so hard, John. She didn't leave to escape you; I think she just needed her freedom."

"But seven *years* . . . ."

"Come on, be a man. Consider what's best for her. I have the means to —"

"I know." John's head bowed in resignation. "You'll treat her right?"

"Better'n any other bird dog in Georgia."

Did the bit of misdirection in "Georgia Peach" work for you? Notice there's only one brief line of interruptive narrative. Could the story be made better with more narrative? Does the setting matter, for example? Does it matter that we don't know the identity of the other character?

The Report

Our ship landed softly, unlike that of my unlucky friend. His lost power and crashed near the place called Corona. I shape-shifted, became a young woman, less frightening than a golden orb sprinkled with stars.

Two approached, and I took them aboard. He seemed tough, but she was tender and sweet.

Both were delicious.

What components of suggestion are at work in "The Report"? Does the fact that the last sentence is in a paragraph by itself add a touch more drama?

Rough Odds

> Walt flicked a butt into the rough.
> "You still smoking?"
> "It's the fastest way to a sure grave, right Doc?"
> "And?"
> "I'm bettin' bein' hit by a bus or a bolt of lightnin' is quicker."
> "Yeah, right." They both laughed.
> Walt took a direct hit from a lightning bolt. Doc shot par, but Walt won.

In "Rough Odds" Walt introduces us to his golfing partner. Is the partner's identity important? Why or why not?

The Mysterious Case of Harlan the Hippie

> The car flipped, landing upside down in a ditch. But being high has its advantages.
> Harlan climbed out, surveyed the scene, then got behind the wheel again, thinking how cool it was to have the world on his back.
> When the officers arrived, the earth was gone, toted off on the roof of Harlan's car.

I've found over the past several years that "The Mysterious Case of Harlan the Hippie" works well for some and doesn't work at all for others. It's another attempt at surrealism, albeit perhaps more as a function of Harlan's being high than depending on a mixture of imagination and reality. Then again, maybe the world really *was* gone . . . .

Finally, one more example in the *Harlan the Hippie* series. This is another attempt at surrealism:

Harlan the Hippie's Snowboarding Mishap

The snowboard flipped through a dimensional vortex, carrying Harlan with it.

Cool! he thought, then lay very still, which seemed the right thing to do. Hearing voices, he glanced past his toes, saw a bevy of snowboards racing toward him.

"Here it is!" one shouted, then climbed aboard Harlan and raced down the slope.

A Few Pointers and Some Exercises

I'd feel a little foolish penning a summary for a chapter on flash fiction, so instead I'll give you a few pointers that didn't fit elsewhere in the chapter and a few exercises to get your thought processes moving.

If you're aiming for a particular word length, say 55 words, it sometimes helps to write on a pad on which the lines are numbered (or number them yourself). Then write *down the left side of the page*, one word per line. When you've reached the bottom of the page, begin at the top again, say in the center of the page. You can easily monitor your word count, and replacing individual words with better ones is a snap.

Use strong, action verbs whenever possible. Use few or no linking verbs (i.e., *became*) and state-of-being verbs (*am, is, are, was, were, be, being, been*). This will reduce your dependence on descriptive adjectives and adverbs, often unnecessary in tight writing and certainly undesirable when words are at a premium. In fact, if you go back and look, you'll find very few adjectives or adverbs in any of the flash fiction pieces above.

Avoid trying to tell the reader everything. Use suggestion (implication) and inuendo instead and *trust the reader to see the scene*. Experiment, experiment, experiment. Write, write, write!

Here are a few flash fiction exercises to get you started:

1. Write a story about a conflict between a man and a woman; two men; two women.

2. Write a story about a conflict between a man and a child; a woman and a child.

3. Write a story about euthenasia; suicide; murder.

4. Write a story about a being from Jupiter; another solar system; another galaxy.

5. Write a story about a conflict between a man and a machine; a woman and a machine; two machines (either "real" or futuristic — mechanical, electric, electronic).

6. Write a story about a conflict or the relationship between two inanimate objects (a cup and the desk it's sitting on; grass and dirt; your shoe and your sock).

7. Write a story about a conflict between a man and an animal; a woman and an animal; two animals.

8. Write a story about a conflict among three people (any gender or mix of genders).

9. Write a story about a conflict between seemingly complimentary professionals (a cop and a lawyer, a baker and a cook, a writer and an editor, a teacher and a principal).

10. Write a story about a conflict between insects; an insect and a boy or girl, man or woman; an insect and his environment; an insect and an unnatural environment.

11. Write a story about an internal conflict of morals (one character).

12. Write a story about a graveyard at midnight; a photo of a deceased relative that the protagonist loved and/or hated.

13. Write a story about a conflict between two or more people in a photograph.

Final Notes

I'd planned to include a section of possible markets for your flash fiction, but the market for any kind of fiction is volatile. By the time this book goes to print, any listing would more than likely be obsolete. Then I considered dedicating a page on my website to a listing of markets, but since a website is sometimes a day-to-day proposition, I decided instead to simply suggest you key "flash fiction" into your search engine and follow the links. When I keyed that phrase into a popular search engine this morning, I was pleased to find this statement across the top of the screen: *Results 1-10 of about 24,200. Search took 0.12 seconds.*

As you surf the various sites, you'll notice there is considerable confusion regarding flash fiction. Some of the venues even mention "flash fiction or short-short stories" as if those phrases are synonymous. They are not. Most short-shorts are up to 1,000 words or so. True flash fiction has space only for a single conflict and a resolution. I recommend you follow a discerning eye when submitting your work to any market, of course, but especially beware the ones that seem not to know the art.

In addition to whatever markets you discover through your web search for "flash fiction," remember that many flash fiction stories are the right length to serve as fillers for magazines. Another possible market is any fiction venue that does not specify a minimum word count in their guidelines. Finally, literary journals almost always are a good venue for flash fiction.

No matter your genre, if you submit your work for publication more than likely you eventually will encounter an editor that is less than encouraging, and maybe even discourteous. As a writer, poet, and editor, I've been on both sides of the editorial fence. By way of a final note, let me remind you to maintain your perspective. After all

You are a writer.
If there were no editors, you would still write.
If there were no writers, what would editors do?

Glossary

Antagonist Usually a well-rounded character who is assigned one or more bad or evil character traits with which we can immediately identify (his type) plus a few unique traits; he is most often the villain.

Barrage The delivery, by one character, of an uninterrupted string of statements, exclamations, or questions for the purpose of conveying to the reader the sense that the recipient of the barrage is being berated or otherwise overwhelmed.

Character A player in the story. A character might be animate or inanimate and might deliver dialogue, receive dialogue, or both.

Conflict The source of tension in a story, in which one or more characters are pitted against one or more other characters or against the situation itself.

Dialogue A character's spoken communication between himself and two or more other characters, or unspoken communication (thought).

Dialogue, realistic Dialogue that is delivered with the spontaneity and free rhythms of everyday speech, so that it serves to further the reader's suspension of disbelief and immerse him more deeply in the story line.

End punctuation *See punctuation, long-pause.*

Interrupting the barrage A tension-heightening technique in which one character attempts to disarm a *barrage* by interruption, the indication of which is the em dash.

Narrative Non-dialogue text that advances the story line while maintaining or heightening reader interest.

Narrative, introductory Non-dialogue text that introduces dialogue and creates or maintains reader interest by providing details that color the ensuing dialogue. Often used in place of the *tag line*.

Narrative, interruptive Non-dialogue text that interrupts dialogue to help provide a sense of ongoing action and the natural rhythms of human speech. Like *introductory narrative*, interruptive narrative also can heighten tension and reader interest by providing details.

Phonetic spelling Spelling a word or phrase, with or without the aid of an apostrophe, to approximate pronunciation in a particular dialect or speech pattern, as "gonna" for "going to" or "should've" for "should have" or (more rarely) "couldn't've" for "couldn't have."

Plot That interlocking series of cause-and-effect *conflicts*, increasing in intensity and tension, that lead, eventually, to the resolution of the story.

Protagonist Usually a well-rounded character who is assigned one or more good or heroic character traits with which we can immediately identify (his *type*) plus a few unique traits; he is most often the hero.

Punctuation, long-pause The period, question mark, exclamation point and colon, most often used at the end of a complete sentence. Also called *end punctuation*.

Punctuation, medium-pause The semicolon, em dash, ellipsis, and sometimes parentheses. In dialogue, the semicolon is most often used to connect two closely related complete thoughts; the em dash to indicate an interruption; and the ellipsis either to indicate halting speech or, when used at the end of a sentence of dialogue, to indicate a voice that is trailing off. The parens is seldom used in dialogue.

Punctuation, short-pause The comma.

Punctuation, spelling Those marks of punctuation that do not create a pause: the apostrophe, the double quotation marks, and the hyphen.

Reader speed The velocity with which a reader is transported through a word or sentence or passage by the writer's intentional use of various combinations of letters, words, and punctuation.

Resolution The satisfactory culmination of the story, usually the final few pages of a novel, paragraphs of a short story, sentences of flash fiction.

Sound length The amount of time it takes to pronounce, aloud or mentally, the sound of a letter or combination of letters. For example, *B* is pronounced faster than *S* or *TH*. This measurement is constant, and it is dependent only on the relative position of the other letter(s) in the word. Because this trait is carried by the letters into words and sentences, it becomes an important tool for subliminally conveying the characters' emotions.

Stereotype A general character type, most often indicated by assignment of a series of traits popularly (and erroneously) believed peculiar to a particular group. Usually used to describe a group of people from a particular race, religion, or geographical area. For example, because of the drawn-out speech patterns exhibited by many who live in the South, Southerners are believed slow witted by some. That belief is based on a *stereotype*.

Truncated Cut short. Using an apostrophe in place of a letter or syllable to shorten a word to create a particular effect in the reader, most often to create the illusion of dialect.

Type, character The general, stereotypical personality with which we immediately identify. The blond or brunette, five foot two-three-four mother of two or three who serves as president of the PTA and drives a minivan is a *type*.

Volleying   Two or more characters going at each other in dialogue without interruption or with only occasional interruption, a technique used to create or expand tension and heighten the reader's emotional experience.

Wandering off-topic   Just as in real life, one or more characters might wander off the original topic of conversation, usually to a related topic, before eventually coming back to the topic.

Contact Information

If you should need clarification of anything in this book at any time, please feel free to contact me at hmpeditor@hotmail.com or harveystan@yahoo.com. I'll do my best to help. Please also feel free to contact me directly with any comments, criticisms, or concerns. I'd especially appreciate any testimonials regarding how this book has helped your writing, as well as any topic or subtopic that you feel I've omitted and should have addressed. Finally, I hope you'll visit my website at http://www.stonethread.com/

About the Author

Harvey Stanbrough is a poet, essayist, and fictionist. Collections of his poetry have been nominated for the Pulitzer Prize, the Frankfurt Award, and the *Inscriptions Magazine* Engraver's Award. He has taught Writing Realistic Dialogue and Writing Flash Fiction at writers' conferences and in private and public seminars. He works as a full-time freelance editor from a farm near Pittsboro, Indiana, and regularly speaks at writers' conferences around the nation.

Index